BEYOND

THE

TETHERED

ROSES

Where

Nothing

Goes

To

The

Grave

A

Memoir

written

by

Trul'ee Benevolence

A

Sequel to:

Changes not Seen..Were hidden in plain sight

&

Taming The Rage Inside; to break Barriers

BUT FOR THE GRACE OF GOD, THERE GO I.

IF YOU ARE OR KNOW SOMEONE WHO IS EXPERIENCING A MENTAL HEALTH CRISIS, PLEASE CALL 988 OR GO TO YOUR LOCAL EMERGENCY ROOM

OR

IF YOU ARE IN NEED OF A DRUG AND ALCOHOL FACILITY OR JUST NEED TO TALK, PLEASE CALL 988 OR GO TO YOUR LOCAL EMERGENCY ROOM.

OR

IF YOUR DEALING WITH DOMESTIC VIOLENCE, PLEASE CALL 1-800-799-7233

AND KNOW, THAT YOUR NOT ALONE!

Copyright 2008

~ Ω ~

....

CONTENTS

Preface: I would like to give honor to God

Chapter 1. The truth nature of things...8

Chapter 2. Reclaiming my life...13

Chapter3. Misjudged...18

Chapter4. The unfortunate truth...23

Chapter 5. My perception...25

Chapter 6. The company we keep...30

Chapter 7. Forgive my shortcomings...38

Chapter 8. Maintaining the balance...48

Chapter 9. Alone in my joy...60

Chapter 10. In spite of...63

Thank You, my dear friend...Tan H.

Too Sustain

You've mastered how to hide the pain behind your smile.
While taking the time to admire the passion hidden inside.

Stuffing your feelings with words not said, trying not to offend, in an attempt to hold on to those loved instead.

While guarding, protecting each step of the way, still monitoring each word you say. Pondering the memories of yesterday, while suffering in silence along the way

How can I express feelings that she will always treasure.

How do I convince her, that what she's gone through isn't forever.

And that she's stronger than the words said to her, that left her the aggressor.

As the silence wisp through the open space, it leaves an unsettling feeling that's far from grace.

That she who sleeps in the midst of fire, has dreams of hate, pain and unnatural desires.

Pivoting on thoughts that form in her wicked head, knowing that she said everything she meant and meant everything she said.

While trying to convince yourself, that you have the ability to push past this pain, take control of your feelings and tap into the good that still remains

All so you can stake your claim

And know, that the she in me does not have to feel the need to be loved, TOO SUSTAIN

TB

Preface

I would like to give honor to God.

Writing this trilogy has been quite a journey. Reaching back in the past to pick and choose which traumatic episode to share with you, {there were many} to re-live each horrific moment after another was exhausting and emotional, to say the least. The origin of these books were from journals that my sponsor suggested that I began writing. Ultimately, there was so much buried inside, that when I begin to write it turned into a memoir. I thought, this would also be a good way to inform my children as to who I am and why. I felt that this would be to much to uncover in a mere conversation so.....

All of my young life with my mother, she never took the time to share stories about her childhood nor her teen years. And when ask, I was told to go away. Everything was a secret back then. I didn't want this for my children because these secrets affected me in a way that I wouldn't wish on anyone. Feeling empty and without worth, leaving me to have questions all of these years gone by, without answers. The idea is to alleviate doubt about my childhood in hopes that these books can explain any questions my boys may have about me. It saddens me, that I had a childhood of this magnitude to share with them however, in their own time, I would hope that if there were any questions or any doubt as to why I did this or that, these books will shed light. In the meantime, I pray that they would charge my head and not my heart.

 May God lay hands on those reading these books to bring them through, to the light as he has for me......... In The Name Of Jesus

Prologue

Let The Truth Be Told

Living in an ERA where adults believed that a child should be seen and not heard. Questions ask, went unanswered, where lies turned secrets, that were never to be told. Fathers missing from the family dynamic, so that mothers could feed the little ones with what little the government provided. Schools were institutionalized, where punishments were made barbaric. Using paddles made from wood and thick plexiglass, that had holes in them that seem to suck the skin inward with each blow. Handles, that were shaped to the punisher's preference. Growing up in a community where men didn't see little girls as such. Just devalued property and behind closed doors, found the means to defile and desecrate them, when at all possible. Where danger, doubt and distrust of a the male species played a big part in a child's life, whether they were male or female. Local restaurants, corner stores and long sharks were all a part of an experiment gone wrong. Where pimps, players and prostitutes went hand in hand. Hustlers and panhandlers stood on every corner along side the ladies of the night. Hot houses, whore houses, gambling and pool halls, where a breading ground for the up and coming ladies of the night, where a blind eye was always turned. And bless the child that has his own, was made a cliche. All alley's in the area that turned into a shortcut home, was meant to find, men crouched down throwing dice up against a brick wall under a lit lamppost. To see fights breakout over the game, they called craps. Vials and baggies seen on the ground with known paraphernalia in them. Prostitutes exiting from dark spaces, looking both ways as if looking for traffic. Where everything seen by a young girl at night, was like being at a carnival with all of the bright lights and known attractions, and people walking everywhere playing the game called life. How were we to live through that, and be unscathed. Truth Be Told.

NOW, I'M GOING TO JUMP AROUND A BIT, SO KEEP UP!

Chapter 1

The true nature of things

Her name was Kathy, I met her on line. We talked and enjoyed each others conversation for at least two months or so. On a Friday evening, she called to ask if I could pick her up from a pilot truck stop on Brick road the next day. She explained that her car was at her apartment, it didn't matter to me, I was happy to oblige. When I pulled up the next day, she walked out with one of the biggest smiles on her face. I couldn't believe how beautiful she was, in person. I told myself that I need to concentrate and not make a total fool of myself. As time passed, she and I became close, so close that I took a week off work, to ride around the country with her in an eighteen wheeler. Never in my wildest dreams had I thought that I would have done this. She took care of me, in the way that I'd hoped, she would. I learned things that I never cared about before.

On the second night, she ask an odd question; are you familiar with bondage? With a puzzled look, No, I answered. She gestured for me to hand her, her phone. She googled, and there it was, a woman tied up and gagged. I stared at this photo for a while until, she finally broke my gaze. She laughed, at my ignorance. Because of how stunned I seemed to be, over something that is so practiced in this country; according to her. She educated me further about the language used for this practice and ask that I study this. As I read further, I looked up to ask; why? She admitted, that she's in to this. Which made me look up into her beautiful eyes and notice that little girl in me shouted; RUN! I couldn't, I was intrigued.

I've always enjoyed applying a little pain by smacking a woman on the ass or nibbling on the nipple or anything else that the woman desired or would allow. But to tie them up and sexually torture them?......I was her student and she my tutor and for the remainder of the week, I learned well. She and I would practice on how, when and where to apply a sexual pleasure, that she desired of course. I aimed to please her, as she has mentally stimulated me. I watched the road ahead and noticed the sign above read South Bend airport. She and I road back to my home with smiles plastered on our faces. I could only believe that it was because of the awesome time spent together. The night was spent, with candles burning and her naked body laying in my arms as we drifted off to sleep.

The next evening, she came over for dinner. I cooked smothered steak with onions and gravy, poured over a potatoes with carrots and peas on the side. I happily watched as she ate it all. I got up to secure the house and rushed back. I gently pulled at her fingers until I had her hand in mine. She and I went downstairs and stood on the bottom steps, while she allowed me to nibble on her lips. I led her to the bed and watched as she made her way to comfort. I then put on some smooth jazz and lit a few candles. She looked even more angelic against the flickering of the candle lights, as she did in the daylight. I creep back to her and slowly peeled her clothes off of her body. Carefully paying attention to every curve while gently kissing and caressing her as if she were a note being played by the tip of my tongue. She is, even more beautiful to me then she was when we first met. I wanted to hold her nakedness in my arms for as long as she would allow. Minutes later, she turned to kiss me and this aroused me in a way that I hadn't been in a while. I slowly moved from her lips to her navel and on to her curvy hips, finding my way to her sweet spot. I massaged it until I hear her ask for it…It was already on board. Slowly, I inserted the head, while working the rest into the tightness of her abyss. After listening to her moan, I moved in more and more, until I was close to climaxing. Her cries, were fuel to my fire. I gave it to her, with long and strong strokes, until I hear her say... look at me. I continued, slowly gyrating. She then gently touched both sides of my face, bringing my lips closer to hers as she ask, again, will you look at me while, making love to me, please.

I looked into her beautiful face, studying her, to gauge her sincerity. I don't quite know where this is coming from. Love was not what I was making, I was fucking her. What she was asking of me, I had trouble doing. Only because I assumed, that making love to her, would mean to actually love her, and that I didn't. "I then realized that I hadn't made that connection with another person since… her. I pulled out, kissing her face, not to admit my disability. Do you remember what I taught you; she ask. Yes; I answered. I reached over and grabbed a small piece of rope and realized, I didn't want to do this with her. I could hurt her or even worse. I could bruise her fair skin enough to cause a concern to someone in her life, that could possibly call the police, I thought. I explained that I wasn't ready for this, she was kind enough to let me off the hook. She allowed me to hold her in my arms until we fell asleep.

The next morning, I watched as she walked to her car. I waved goodbye and turned to walk into the kitchen. Before I crossed the threshold, there was a knock at the door. It was her, with tears in her eyes. She explained; it's not you, it's me. I'm no good for you; she said. Baby, your perfect; I told her, not truly believing what's happening, here. I'm no good, she said. What do you mean? I ask. You did nothing wrong, I'm just all wrong for you, she added. As she turned to walk out, I held her hand in mine, as she slipped from my grip, I watched as she walk out of my life. I tried calling her, no answer. Texting, no response. I wondered and worried about her, every day after that. Going back and forth in my head, wondering what I had done, was it this or that. As time passed, I realized that I was really feeling her. Never again, will this shit happen to me; I shouted!

Sitting at my desk, looking out to see the neighbor's children playing with their rambunctious dog, named Frock. I know this because, they've had to call him many times in the past. I noticed, the mailman coming in the distance, close enough now to notice that, he is a she, today. As I stood from where I sat. I see that frock has ran into the street. I smiled as I watched the kids run out to retrieve him. My mother instinct kicks in, as I look both ways, checking for cars. I move towards my bedroom door to I hear a noise coming from the rear of the house. As I move toward the kitchen, I can now hear rustling, what in the fuck? I mumbled. Loud enough now, that it has my full attention. I moved slowly in the direction of where the noise was coming from, only to realize that it's coming from a bedroom near the back door. I stopped right outside of the door and slowly placed my ear against it, in hope that I could hear the noise again, just to pin point where it's coming from, before I go in. I slowly opened the door, just enough to see what could possibly be stirring around in here. I quietly walked in and looked in the closet, nothing. I then knelt down to glance under the bed, still nothing. As I stood to my feet, I heard a moan as if, someone who's in distress.

I slowly walked further in and stood by the edge of the bed, to see that she was still there, in bondage, just as I left her. On her hands and knees, with her legs crossed at her ankles, that were tied together. Her arms brought back on the sides of her body strategically tied to her ankles as well. This position, left her long clitoris visible and available to me. I removed the black ball blocking the entrance to her mouth and watched as a dribble of saliva fell from her juicy lips to the sheets beneath her. When she said nothing, I quickly put it back and made my way to the foot of the bed, to see that her pussy was pulsating. I could see that there was a small amount of juice exiting her vagina. I licked two of my fingers and slowly touched the spot where I felt, would get the most response. I then, slowly ran my fingers from her clitoris to her anus and then back again finding my way inside. While watching, as she responded by moving her hips. She then let out a scream through the side of her gag, until I said, STOP! All movement ceased. As I continued, I could hear a slight whimper escape. I pulled out of her quickly, watching as her body jerked. As she slowly came to relax, I went back in, pulled out again. I walked around the bed slowly, tugging at the ropes that held her, to make sure that they weren't too loose or too tight. I walked back to the head of the bed and pulled the black ball from her mouth again, to watch her seductively lick away the juices that fell from her lips, as it did before. She hesitated before speaking; I want more mistress, please; she blurted out. When I'm ready, I said sternly. I put the ball back into her mouth and continued to check the house for strangers. When I returned, I gave her all that she ask for and more. When the deed was done, I removed the ropes, kissed her on the forehead, telling her that she did a great job, ran a bath and washed, oiled and massaged her bruised body.

When I became a lesbian, my intentions were to treat all women unlike any man had ever treated me. I vowed never too harm a woman in the way that I had been harmed. The objective, was to show love and do good and that, I have done. However, there are women who practice this thing. This thing, that I've always thought was a malfunction within my brain. As I said before, I've found pleasure in tapping a little ass or pinching a nipple or two, which I thought was a form of foreplay. However, after being informed as to what this was, I began educating myself, further. I now know, that this is called BDSM. Which sounds worse, than it really is. But in hindsight, I aim to please them in any way, that they wish.

I've always felt emotionally detached from those who have shown a certain level of dominance or somewhat of an authoritarian figure, over women. Those who rule over others, were just not cool in my book. But recognizing, who I've become today and the many justifications I've made up in my mind for it, has become redundant. It felt safe, being able to mentally and emotionally withdraw from groups of people in that way. It kept me from having to see myself, in them. However, working with these ladies, bringing them pleasure, puts me in control with what is going on, in the space that we occupied. This, also makes me responsible for my actions. Now, as time passed. I developed habits that kept me safe from the pain and disappointment of being in a real relationship or friendship, for that matter. I eventually learned how to properly and positively incorporate coping techniques, that actually worked for me at the time. While realizing, that I was just substituting one addiction for another. Because of these behaviors, my psychiatrist deemed me to be, an Introvert. Not quite knowing what this meant, at the time. I had an immediate rebuttal, only because I thought that she was speaking ill of me. However, after educating myself, maybe she was right. With the exception of my children, the need for those small entities were far and between. That was only a portion of what I felt, could be wrong with me.

Chapter 2

Reclaiming my life

Looking at the contour of her face. Searching for a change in her expression, as I share bits and pieces of my life with her. With every twist and turn that I take her on, she sit motionless, expressionless, as if nothing that I've said, affected her in any way. I'm not sure if I'm mad about it, or offended. I wanted empathy, maybe a bit of sympathy for my money but she showed none. Every time, that I leave Miss Levey's office, after having a therapy session, I feel exhausted, to the point that I need a nap. Struggling through what I feel comfortable sharing and what I actually share, takes a tole on me. I never really share on the shit, that I should have. Conversation about my mother, were always off the table. I was much too ashamed to speak to anyone about our relationship, let alone a therapist. I had memories of things said to me by her, that I couldn't bring up, from where they were buried in my head, anyways. God forbid, she or anyone else tell me, to let it go. My question to them would be, How? I've carried this shit around with me for most of my life, tucked away in a safe place, so that I can move forward with my life.

Slowly making my way through traffic. I thought of a memory that I shared with her today, about my son Darion's graduation from high school. He broke my heart that day. When ask, who was the person or persons responsible for you being where you are today? In front of an auditorium full of other graduates, teachers and guests, he answered; his father. And only, his father. I knew this not to be true, as well as the rest of my family, who sit beside me. I'm aware of the anger that he felt towards me, for something that I wasn't able to do for him because I had to work, some months earlier. But, to chose to punish me in this way, was something unexpected. However, the fact remains, he lied. This held me bound for a while. I knew that he was a spoiled child. Only because, during the time that he grew up, I was working and drug free, so he reaped the benefits of it all. "I had no idea that it would come back to bite me, in my ass." Later, speaking to his father, he expressed his surprise as well.

However, I came to the conclusion years ago, through many sessions of therapy, that my trauma became their trauma by way of association. However, for what ever reason, I lived in the illusion that I was shielding them from it all.

My children were adults now. I still felt a need to provide those things for them, that I felt, weren't provided for me as a young adult. I'm sure that subconsciously, my motive was to make up for all of the wrong, that I had done when they were younger, which made sense to me. When I got clean and sober and realized that I could stay clean and sober with the help of NA, AA and CA, life became much more manageable. I started with giving them quality time. Again, because as child my parents gave me as little as possible. Money, was as it came, it went, living paycheck to paycheck wasn't easy. However, I was very resourceful. And as it's said, I could make a dollar out of fifteen cents. I was always cool, calm and collective with the women that I encountered. When possible, I was accommodating and straight forward. I took pride in always being honest with them, which gave them a choice to decide if they wanted what I had to offer. Giving head, was one thing that I wasn't able to provide, for safety reasons, of course. However, the hustle was real and my creativity was in full affect to substitute, so there were no disappointment. I was blessed to have been in the company of some very generous women. It was an unspoken agreement, that I was there to provide a service for them and in turn. … I thought that my boys may have known what was going on, and could have had an issue with it but, because this didn't interfere with their day to day, it wasn't a problem.

Trying to maneuver my way through life wasn't easy for me back then. Nor, was it easy for those that came across my path, that wanted hear the word, love, from me. I heard that word spoken many times in the past, but their actions didn't match the definition. I felt that I was incapable of loving, I wasn't responsible for the love that they claim to have for me. In the two years of being without a partner, I've seen some of my friends go from one relationship, where they said, they were madly in love with one and go right into another and feel that same type of love for the other. As I have told Yvette and anyone who would listen at the time; she was the only person that I had ever fallen in love with. And don't believe that I will ever fall in love again. I not only loved her, I loved the family dynamic that we shared. Of course, I had a small amount of hope and even prayed for a relationship after ours but maybe I wasn't ready I guess, or maybe not with the women that I was with at the time. I always, wore a smile that assured everyone that I was in a good space, OK so to speak. Laying down with women and getting up without feeling was nothing for me. I protected my heart at all cost. Being called a pimp by some and a whore monger by other didn't matter either. I was unaffected by others opinion of me and how I, do me. But, as resilient as my children have proven to be throughout my indiscretions. I sometimes felt that as long as my actions weren't affecting their growth, then that's all that mattered to me.

With time, came growth. Still enjoying the company of a woman. I began to stimulate my mind more, with other things that life had to offer. Those things that weren't at my grasp before. Posted on a wall, was a flier of a play that the Notre Dame students were putting on. Which was a production of Romeo and Juliet, there on campus. I went with a young lady that didn't appreciate it but I loved their adaptation. Which was just a ripple in my small pond. I then, began to notice that the longer that I stayed single, the more time on my hands that I had, to learn. I chose to gain knowledge of thing that were new to me. I began going to black plays and concerts at the Morris performing arts center, as well. I also noticed friends who had become family, going their separate ways for frivolous reasons. For instance, one of my friends were angry with me about someone that I had a fling with, this person wasn't even a part of our circle. But, because the female had been with another friend of "my friend" she expressed loudly that I needed to keep my dick in my pants. I thought it was a joke, so did others that heard her, however I quickly found that it wasn't. In disbelief, most of our friends, felt that they had to make a choice based on the length of time known each of us. Well, that choice wasn't me. The others (and there were many of us) had gotten into new relationships and because I was single, I didn't quite fit in or in some cases, there were trust issues. Whatever the case may have been, I've never crossed the line with any of my friends, nor those who were just curious.

It was a bunch of bullshit, I say. I've never been a person to force myself on anyone. In denial, tried to reach out to some of them a few times and nothing. However, I noticed that they were all still meeting up with out me. I knew then that my time with them was done. This, hurt to the core. I now had to stuff this way down deep with the rest, to muffle the pain. Soon after, I met new people. Remembering that saying; "when one door closes, another will open." In this journey with these new friends or associates, I find myself working hard, at an attempt to emulate what looked like friendships, although difficult for me. Realizing that it takes me longer to trust.

I got on the highway and drove 1 hour and 20 minutes. I pulled up to my destination and sit. Psyching myself up, I finally got out and went up, to knock on the door. There she stood in the doorway in a very revealing long black two piece negligee with shoes to match. She looked stunning to be a 62 year old woman. I planted a kiss on her cheek as I passed. I slowly removed my coat and watched as she removed it from my hand. When she returned, I grabbed her around her waist and pulled her close. Before her next breath, I passionately kissed her lips while slowly moving my right hand down the curves of her body, to find her sweet spot. Once there I noticed how incredibly moist it was, she inhaled when she felt my fingers fondling her insides. She began to breath harder as I twirled around just inside the opening of her pussy and pulled out abruptly. The disappointment, on her face was priceless, this fed my desire for her. I instructed her to go to her room, she turned and did as she was told. When I made it to the top of the stairs. I peeped in to see, that every pleasure toy that she desired for this session was neatly arranged on the stand, as I had ask. She was an intelligent woman, that knew exactly what she wanted. I enjoyed watching her response to everything that I did to her.

When I walked back in from washing my hands, I noticed that the ropes around her wrist were slipping off, I noticed that she still held the position, As I reached up to tighten them, she leaned back against me as if she wanted more of what I gave her earlier. I then positioned myself behind her, prying her legs apart, lubed up and went inside of her pounding and pounding, until I heard her shout;

RED! I pulled out slowly, in an attempt to get the reaction that I undoubtedly received. I began to playfully smack her on the cheek of her ass and then rub it for comfort. I then did the same with the other side. This seemed to get no response from her. I then, removed the whip from the stand and put it to her backside. I rubbed it against her skin, teasing her. I then proceed to spank her, alternating from one cheek to the other until I heard, RED! Again. Panting as if out of breath, I then gently massaged the welts that were forming. She looked at me with puppy dog eyes, not saying a word as I instructed. I brought her down from the pole, laid her across the bed and left out to run her a shower. When I returned, she was laying on the floor on top of a narrow piece of plastic. I could only imagine the confused look on my face. I will pay you $500.00 to give me golden showers; she said. What is that? I ask. I want you to pee on me, silly, she said, with a smile on her face. Oh, hell No, baby! I said abrutly. No! No! No!; I added, as I turned and walked in the bathroom. This shit is crazy, I mumbled to myself, as I walked back out. Thinking about the money, I ultimately gave this woman, what she ask for. I felt numb inside afterwards, what did I just do? She has always appreciated my services as I have always appreciated her generosity. I reached over and put the $2,000 in my wallet. I then gently and quietly cleaned her body. Finally, to lay next to her, holding her in my arms, until we fell asleep.

The ride home, I was in deep thought about what I had done, back there. Is this who I've become? What else would I be willing to do for that, oh mighty dollar? ask the left side of my brain. But, because I came into this world broke, it doesn't mean that I have to remain broke, says the right side of my brain. This is crazy, I spoke out loud, as if talking to both sides of my brain. I pride myself on being a person that would never hurt a woman the way that I had been hurt. But I am; I answer myself. Only at their request, or with their permission. I feared that when I look back thirty years from now, the she, in me, will still exist.

I pulled up in front of the house, and just sit for a moment, to speak words of affirmation into the universe before going in. "From this day forward, my goal will be to hold myself accountable for my actions, and to show love and do good, no matter the circumstance."

As I walked through the door, I noticed just how quiet it was, and realized, this is just how I like it. Peace is my purpose today. I stopped in front of the closed door next to my bedroom and knocked, waited and then opened it to see that Jeremiah is still in the bed at 2pm in the afternoon. He's a preteen now and is lazy as his brothers were. It's time to let go of that bed and get some work done around here, young man; I said, playfully. He moaned under his covers as he stretched and yawned. He's grown quite a bit taller than I thought he would. He's gotten darker as well and his hair isn't as curly as it was, when he was younger. I can recall the agency putting on his paperwork that he was a mixed child. Which is why, I chose my friend Trish to be his God mother. She had a many attributes; she fished, hunted and built things. I don't believe there was anything that she couldn't do. I felt that she could teach him more about the caucasian side of him than I could. She was amazing with him. She made sure to be in our lives, every chance that she had.

She rode her motorcycle from Wisconsin to see us. It rained 70 miles out but she kept riding through. To be honest, she was more of a friend to me, than I was to her. It wasn't anything that she had done, it was me, and how my mind is wired, being afraid to put my whole self in, for fear of being brutally devastated. Seventeen years of friendship, that I felt came about only came about because we lived so far away. In my opinion, if she had been closer, maybe she wouldn't have felt the need.

Chapter 3

Misjudged

Late nights, made early mornings bearable when spent with the right person. She was a true red head, thick around the thighs with eyes as big a round as Bettie Davis. Shy, as I like them. Aiming to please, which made for a good submissive. Her mouth, oh, her mouth was so beautiful, with the shade of lipstick that she wore. Her lips, caressed her beautiful white teeth every time she spoke, which set the pace of the night. My business was my own and sharing my whereabouts wasn't my M.O. however, there were those that felt that because of a time or two spent with me, that they had earned this information. There was a lesson that I learned years ago, never let the right hand know what the left is doing.

The sun crept it's way through the gap in the curtains to find me. In an attempt to avoid the blinding glare, I turned over to see her curvy hips that formed underneath the sheet, This took me back to last night's activities, which put a smile on my face. I reached over to caress her, when the phone rang. I stopped and turned around to answer it. She paused, and then spoke in a stern voice….I know that she's in there. Good morning to you too, I said, as I looked around for my house shoes. Before she could utter another word, we can talk later dear; I said calmly. We don't have too, DEAR! she said with aggression. Her tone tickled me a little. She hung up. I laid back down, to wake her with a kiss that brought her into my arms. She protested about her breath, but I told her that I didn't smell a thing. I continued until the phone rang again. Hold on a minute baby. Hello; I answered, you might want to get up and look out of your window, she said calmly, and then I heard the dial tone. I turned and kissed her on the forehead and urged her to go and freshen up a bit and I'll be right back. When I heard the bathroom door close, I opened the front door to find Tabitha standing in the middle of the street with tears rolling down her face.

Look what you made me do; she said as the pointed in the direction of a car that was parked in front of my home. I looked over to see an enormous bolder sitting in the middle of Brenda's windshield. How did she lift that thing, I wondered. I immediately looked back, to see if Brenda was coming in my direction. I didn't want her to see this. Why? I whispered to her. She got into her car and drove off, with the look of sadness on her face, leaving me to deal with her shit. Tabitha and I had a thing, for almost as long as I was with my wife. Practicing polygamy wasn't a problem once, there was an understanding between the two. However, as the time passed and Tabitha knew of the breakup between me and the wife, she wanted me, all to herself. But what she didn't know wast, that this was frightening to me. Because she and I together had eleven children which made for a very large family. All that I saw for our future, was poverty. I explained that I couldn't do this, because I wasn't what she needed for her and the kids, she seemed to have taken it well when I said it but…... Three weeks later, here we are.

I closed the front door and slowly walked back into the bedroom to be greeted, with a very warm and beautiful smile. I kissed her face while pulling her into my arms. As I held her close, I struggled with my integrity. I searched my mind for words that I might say, to smooth over what happened to her car, which was all a lie. The more I contemplated and conjured, the farther away from the truth I became. She doesn't have to know that I know how this happened; I thought. Hey sweetie, I have things that I have to get done today, I said, so I'm going to have to take a rain check on round two, OK? The pouted with her pretty pink lips, almost made me change my mind. However, I didn't want it at this point. She and I walked to the door. I pulled her near and kissed her passionately on the lips. I opened the door while flirting with her, kissing her once more while saying my goodbyes. I closed the door and two minutes later, I hear a blood curdling scream, followed by her crying aloud. I opened the door, surprised to see her bent over, holding her stomach as if she was in excruciating pain. She pointed in the direction of her windshield, I looked at it and then her, noticing that her mouth was opened as if to scream, but nothing was coming out. I knew then, that she was hurting badly. I watched, as her tears began flowing profusely. I instantly felt bad as I walked over and looked again, as if for the first time. With arms wide open, I pulled her close to hold her in my arms. I gently pulled her head to my chest and assured her, that I would take care of it. We went back into the house so that I could put on clothes and call around to get prices. There was only one place open on this Sunday and it was, Zebart.

When the gentleman walked out with the estimate, I looked down at it, looked up to the ceiling and smiled, attempting to manage the emotions that were now stirring inside. I signaled for the man to start working on it, turned to her, you can come back to the house to wait, if you like; I said. She looked at me, and said, no, I'm fine.

Leaving me to feel as if there were words left unsaid. I paid the man at the desk, turned to her; if you need me call, OK. Thank you; she said. I left out thinking; $300.00. Now, that was an expensive piece of pussy. I never saw her, again.

I've felt the evil that lurks inside but what I've never felt was jealousy to the degree of destruction. Finally, I heard from Tabitha. After taking the time to listen, as to how hurt and devastated she felt that I left her, brought on feelings of intense exasperation. I pulled in a breath of air and calmly reminded her, that she deserved better than me, that we had to go our separate ways. She cried out. I remained calm and quietly ask; can you please help, by repaying at least half on the damage, that you caused to that girls windshield? Her tears ended abruptly. She laughed, out loud. Her response left me speechless. These were the consequences of your own actions, she said, and walked away. I took that as a definite, No. After all of the time that I've known her, I misjudged her.

There were lessons to be learned from this. I'm not sure that I choose the better. However, my choice was to stay to myself for a while, until I knew in witch direction was best for me. In my mind, I knew the type of person that I wanted to become however, getting there would require time, patience and knowledge, which I felt, I'd wasted so much of. I turned down a few invites to events for a while and focused on learning more about myself. Reading self help books by Iyanla Vanzant and motivational books on how to achieve peace, and countless others on serenity, that were very helpful to my well being. My love for the arts increased as well. While stepping up my knowledge of cultural arts, was a gift given to myself. I felt engaged, enough to find myself at an art gallery in Chicago, that was black owned. I felt empowered as I passed over the threshold. I not only found a way to afford one beautiful painting but went back to acquire yet another. Feeling the world shift beneath my feet was quite an invigorating experience. Loosing all of my friends seemed to be a blessing in disguise. I moved different, I felt different, not better than but different, and when I stepped out on the town again, I was alone but felt surrounded by a spiritual entity.

Other than my children, I had two people who chose to stay in constant contact with me. I thanked them often for their consistency, and apologized for my lack of. I still struggled with trust issues, that I work on daily. Putting all of my energy into a person, was just a difficult task for me. I seem to feel safe when I stay my distance. Natasha, is one of those people that I had known for a few years. Due to the fact that, she dated someone that I once called a best friend. Because of the pain that this ex-friend caused, I stepped away, never to return. Natasha, hung in there with me and we slowly, became friends. She found love again. She was happy to introduced me to her new boo, whose name was Donna. She seemed a bit stand offish towards me in the beginning however I felt that when she gets to know me better, she'll warm up. There was a small group affiliated with knowing them as well, which was OK because, I knew them from years earlier but again, they were their friends.

Fast forward…... After five years of kicking it with them. I thought that it would be cool, if we all went on vacation together. They would always talk about wanting to travel, in the way that I do. However, this idea was forgotten about, as time went by. Now, after all of this time of knowing each other, Donna still hadn't quite warmed up to me, as I had thought she would. I may have been partially responsible for this, only because of the way, she moved when around me. I could feel that she wasn't feeling flava. I never did feel comfortable being around people while in their relationships much, for this very reason. As I've seen in the past, the male or the male figure {stud} would have a problem with my hanging around as often, so I didn't. However, I would come when invited, Natasha always made sure that if there was something going on, I knew about it. I'm not quite sure that Donna cared for that. I could sometime tell, by the way she moved, when near me and the silence that incur.

Chapter 4

The unfortunate Truth

Five hours and some change is how long it took me to drive from South Bend to Wisconsin. As soon as Jeremiah and I pulled up in the driveway, we noticed her standing there with a welcoming smile, which made me smile. She seemed so exited that she could hardly contain herself. As we walk in the house, she announced that she wanted to teach Jeremiah how to shoot a riffle. I stopped in my tracks but he's only nine? I said. I looked around her home as I waited for a response, noticing her decor. The fish and camping decorations on the table with the deer antlers mounted, were pretty awesome to look at. It's better that kids learn how to respect a fire arm at an early age, she said. Being from the city, this wasn't as much of a priority to us, as it is to people in the country, I said. Trish took it upon herself to buy him a twelve gauge riffle earlier in the month, without my knowledge.

The next morning was such a beautiful sight, from where I slept. I could see a doe behind a small bush nibbling at the leaves. I lay back down to watch as it moved from one branch to another. Trish walked out on to the porch; how did you sleep out here? She ask. It was really nice, quiet and comfortable, I quickly responded. I hurried to turn my attention back to the doe, to see if she had scared it away. It was still there but my friend kept talking and fucked up the moment. I turned towards her and gave her my undivided attention after that. She then, offered breakfast and proceed to map out our day for us. After breakfast, she leads me into the spare room where my son slept. As I crossed the threshold, I poked fun at the stuffed man sized bear that stood in the corner of the room. I watched as she went into the closet, where there was a six foot tall safe. That when opened, it reveled five rifles and something that I didn't quite recognize. She reached in and pulled out a tall box. It had a picture of a rifle on it. I couldn't believe how real this thing looked as she pulled it out of the box. I watched as she caressed and held it up to admire it. I sit and watched as she reached over, pulled out a dust cloth from the safe and began to caress it, even more. When she finished, we all walked outside to stand, awaiting instructions. She handed it to me first.

 I waited for her instructions, feeling a bit anxious as she began showing me how to hold and handle it. While telling me to hold my breath and when ready, shoot. It's not as if I had never had a firearm in my hands, this weapon was a bit intimidating to me. I was nervous and it was hard for me to retain what little information was given. However, after I fired the gun, I realized that it had a hell of a kick to it. Although it shot pellets, it's kick, in my mind, was too much for my boy. I made her aware of my concerns and she assured me that, she would coach him as to how to hold and handle the rifle properly. I thought for a moment and then, agreed. She was amazing with him. I watched as she made him aware as to how powerful and dangerous this firearm was if he didn't handle it properly, putting great emphasis on the fact that, "it isn't a toy." I noticed the care that she took as she cradled his hand, while showing him where to hold it. Staying near his ear, whispering instructions, showing him how much pressure to apply to the trigger, how to breath and when he was ready, we will let off a round; I heard her say, with excitement. He seemed to be in tune with her. She was patient and very informative. She loaded the gun and prepared him for what was to come and when she felt that he was ready, POW! My attention hurried to his face, I needed to see his face. Hey! I shouted! In a playful manner. How do you feel? He turned slowly, with the biggest smile on his face, I'm good, he said. I was happy for him. They carried on out there for hours, as I took the most endearing and memorable pictures of them with my Cannon camera. I felt, that he was going to leave here knowing much more than we did before we came.

The two of them left the next morning at 5 AM. to go out on her boat, to go fishing. And when they returned that afternoon, she showed him how to properly fillet a fish, which was pretty cool to see. We all, then took a ride down through the back roads of Wisconsin, which were very beautiful. It was time to end a wonderful weekend. As I looked in the rear view mirror to see my son happily playing with his toys, I made my way up the highway. I couldn't help but feel that I was a little responsible for this that I see in him. I ask, are you good? Yes; he said. OK, we are on our way; I whispered. The drive home didn't feel as long as it did on the way there, I had a lot to think about as far as friendships were concerned because, I knew then, that I had a good one.

Chapter 5

My Perception

Friendships turned family, were always important to me, especially when my true family wasn't available, to be family. Still today, I walk through the rooms of different events here in South Bend, and realize that there isn't a soul in the room that is related to me by blood. I understood early on, that religion played a huge part in our division however, my family always thought that prayer was the answer to all that was unholy and or unnatural, in their eyes. But then, I digress.

This new group and I, were going on at least 6 years of friendship. Moving the party from house to house, bar to bar or a park. We mostly partied at Donna and Natasha's home when nothing special was happening elsewhere. While creating memories that were thought to last a life time between us. Still feeling but ignoring, what may have been a little tension between some of us. I remained, only because I wanted their friendships. Now, Tripp was someone that I had know for years through another acquaintance. We spoke, when spoken too but never more than that. However, when we connected through this group, she admitted that she didn't like me, way back when, when ask why? "Because you thought that you were all that." she said, with a straight face. I chose to remain silent and just smiled. She then admitted that she feels differently, now that she's had the chance to get to know me better. I chose to feed her with a long handled spoon, after that conversation. Pearl, doesn't really talk to me but she's cordial. I've know her for a while as well but we've never quite meshed. Avery, is Pearl's wife. I knew her from many years back also but not as well as she says, that she knows me. I just couldn't remember some of the things that she described. I guess, these these memories were from the days when I was coming out of my, drug fog.

Somewhere in or around September of 2017, I had a brainstorm. I thought that it would be a great Idea, if we all planned a Vacation together, this time, as a group. It didn't matter to me, when or where as long as it fell into the next year, where this gave us time to get our finances in order. Natasha, called that same week to invite me over for drinks, which was perfect. All that I could think about was, how I would pitch my idea in a way that would persuade them to go. But when that Friday rolled around, I was informed that the party had been moved to Tripp's, house. I wasn't quite sure about the atmosphere over there because it always seemed a bit louder. When I finally showed up, it was a house full. The party was on. Finally, finding what I felt, was the perfect time, I made my pitch and while under the influence, we all cheered that it was an amazing idea.

When everyone sobered up, we made it official. I then called Trish, to see if she was on board. Hell! Yea! She yelled through the phone. And because I was familiar with cruise ship information. I was the go to person, about any concerns or fears and instructions. There was one thing that I insist on. This, was that they handle their own money transactions. So I decided early on to get a travel agent, make a Facebook page, just to keep everyone in the loop. At the time, I was also in the process of staging my home to be sold. I stayed in constant contact with Trish during this time, she seemed to know much more about these things than I did, although I had a great Realtor. Mrs. Ulnar, came into my home and told me what I needed to do and I followed her instructions to the T. We put the Re max sign in the yard and there was an offer on the table the first week, that the house officially went on the market. I was ecstatic. It was time to pack up and move, although I had no idea where I was going.

Thinking about renting, I looked at some apartments. I then, pictured someone living over my head with little children and quickly thought against it. I then thought of renting a house but eventually decided against it, as well. I put my things in storage and went to stay with my Jamie and Elise and their four children. I saved my money, paid on new furniture, while paying on my cruise at the same time, which was a hell of a juggling act. Trish, made me aware that she too, was selling her home in Wisconsin. She mentioned, that she wanted to move back home, near Elkhart. I was happy for her because, she seemed to have it all worked out. I, on the other hand, was unsure of my journey. But as the weeks turned to months, I moved more towards buying another home. I called and ask my friend Callie if she knew a Realtor that knew this area here in or near Mishawaka. She called back with a number of a woman named Celeste, who had been a family friend of theirs for years. Two weeks had passed and finally, a face to go with the name. I couldn't help but notice right away, how incredibly attractive she was, with this tan that seemed to glow. I told myself that this is about business. Because, I have on occasion, leaped before carefully thinking things through.

The first day we met, she and I, went to look at two homes that didn't quite match up with what I had in mind. However, she stayed consistent. I met her when at all possible for a few months. There were times of course that I would go on the websites and look myself, she would then, pull up the info on the house and we would meet, there. Zillow, had a home available where Mishawaka and South Bend divides. I went over alone to take a look at it, it was so cute. I called Celeste to ask if we could see it, she looked it up and saw that it wasn't for sale. I was disappointed but determined. So I drove a half a mile up the street and there was a 4-sale sign in a yard of a home on the corner. It was quaint but it was a corner lot; I thought out loud. I pulled around the corner, I just had to see the inside of it. I looked around doing a survey of the area. It was clean, quiet and people were jogging and riding bikes. This made me feel pretty good.

With crossed fingers, I walked up on the porch, knocked lightly and waited. A cheerful voice came and stood in the doorway, hi; may I help you? I'm her to inquire about the sign in the yard; I answered. Well, come on in and meet my husband Chuck, my name is Sade; she answered quickly. As I stepped over the threshold; we just put that sign out this morning; she chuckled loudly, from the other room. He walked in from the kitchen with the most inviting smile. Hello; my name is Tru, thank you both for your time. Let me take you on a tour; said Chuck. I smiled and stepped aside to allow him to lead. As we walked through the living room, I was in awe as to how large it was. Finally making it through to the bathroom, I noticed that it had been remolded and they chose the color lavender to put on the walls. I stepped in each of the three bedrooms with him, to notice that they were a nice size, as well. When we turned to leave, I could see that someone smokes quite a bit by the buildup on the ceiling. As he and I continued on, now walking through the kitchen and dinning room area, I could see potential through the clutter. I followed him to the basement and could smell the cigarette smoke even more down there. I listened as he explained everything that he felt was wrong with the house, which wasn't much in my opinion. We walked to the left, going into a spacious laundry room, with a door that lead into a utility room. Which had a door that lead out to the main area. When we came out, we walked across the room to go into another full bathroom with a shower.

As we proceed, I see another room that was a huge open space. I turned to see that all of this was the entire length of the house above. I knew in my heart, that this would be the place were my family would create memories. One more thing that I have to show you; he said with excitement. He and I walked outside in the back yard to see what he knew would sell this home. Although there were neighbors closely surrounding the house, it was quiet, serine, well kept and a perfect place for my family. I gave Celeste the go ahead to file the paperwork for me and them because, the owners moved forward without having a Realtor. When she came back with a yes, she found that the property was actually worth more, than what they ask for. But the sellers stood firm on what we agreed upon. "Look at GOD, I said out loud.

I found that Trish had sold her home and was packed up to come to Elkhart, as well. I told her that I will be there to help unload. When she made it to Elkhart. While we were unpacking, she had an idea that she move in with me and co-parent my son. Wow! I thought to myself. Well it sounds OK but, let's get us all situated first; I said. I didn't quite know what else to say. After two more visits to the house and hearing that everything passed with flying colors, I closed on my second home, in my lifetime, "look at God."

My friend Kissy and her son Rice came in with me after I received the key. They did what a real friend would have done, they help me reconstruct the entire house, upstairs and down to make it mine. It took us thirty one days to turn it around and that we did. Trish, came by near the end, to sand the floors and put the polyurethane down. When everything was all done, I thanked them with hugs, while offering them money, which they wouldn't take. We all went out to sit on the porch to take a break. We were proud of the work done on the house, and it reflected in our conversation. When I noticed the conversation moving towards Trish, living here with me, I evaded the conversation as best as I could. Moving day, lil Jamie, Roland and a few of their friends made it look so easy. My new furniture came in, the next week, which made me very happy. Everything looked amazing. Hats off to Kissy and Rice.

I was ready to talk now, so I called Trish over. But when I opened the door, I couldn't get a word in edgewise. I think, that it would be cool if Jeremiah went deer hunting up north me; she said with a big smile on her face. Deer hunting? I ask. Well, he has the concept of shooting a gun now, all I have to do is help him with the discipline and the patience to sit and wait on his prey; she added. I know that you believe that this is cool but I don't want my son killing animals on my watch, my friend; I said calmly. It won't be on your watch Tru, he's my godson and I wouldn't let anything happen to him; she added with confidence. Well, he is your Godson, however dear, he is my son; I added. The silence in the room was eerie. She looked up from the floor where she had turned her gaze and said, OK. Are you really OK with this? I ask. Yes, I am; she answered sternly. I walked over and hugged her tightly, I held her there for a few more seconds to make sure. As I released her, she whispered, I found a house in the country that I want to buy. OK. I said, with excitement.

Are you sure? Yes, I am; she admitted. Now it was time to focus on the cruise, I thought.

Chapter 6

The Company we keep

There were only six of us going on the cruise, everyone else bailed. Things had finally slowed down enough that I could finally introduce Trish to the rest of the group. I kept in constant contact with them all, through the page that I made on Facebook. Informing them as to when to sign up for their excursions and entertainment on the ship. We had three months left before the date of our cruise and I found that Trish wasn't corresponding. When I called to talk to her, I could feel the tension in her voice. So, I got my son ready and we made the drive to Elkhart, too find out if there was something that I could do or say to fix this.

As I crossed the threshold of her home, I could feel the resistance from her. Hello my friend; I say with a big smile. Hello Tru, she murmur's. Is everything? OK dear; I ask. Yes, she said softly. It was obvious that something about me, was wrong with her. I noticed that you weren't corresponding on the sight. I watched as she sit up as if something startled her. I don't have Wifi; she said with a snarl. Is that even possible? I joked. She looked at me, like "bitch" so I took it down a notch. Trish, you know that if you can't get Wifi on your cell phone out here, you can go to a McDonalds or a library to check the updates for the cruise however, since your in the room with me, I have signed you up for everything already. I reminded her. She was not impressed, I knew that I had to say something to bring her back because if she canceled, I would have to find another roommate, or cancel my cruise. I knew I couldn't afford a balcony suite on my own. So I turned on the charm and finally got her smiling and sharing how things are going in other areas of her life.

When we left her home it was dark out, I was confident that all was well.

In February of 2018, I prepared myself for a long day of travel. We were all to meet at the airport at 3:40 in the am. The limo that I ordered, surprisingly made it on time, to take us all to O'Hare Airport. The ride there was quiet, I could only guess that everyone was tired, so I said a few words and hunkered down for the ride. Finally made it to the airport, we all were attempting too check in on the Kiosk before checking the bags but Tripp was having a very hard time, Trish came to her rescue, though. We then heard her having a conversation about the price of her luggage. She was not happy at all. Once we were all ready and began our stroll too security, I heard her say that she don't have money for this shit. Oh boy; I thought to myself, this is going to be one hell of a trip.

 We exited the plane and walked out to find our shuttle to the hotel. Tripp complained about the prices of a hotel in Florida, as well. I made her aware that, this is why your bunking up with your roommate, she then calmed down. I suggested that we go out to see the town once we all got settled into our room but Natasha wasn't feeling well due to the baby. She and Donna were expecting a child together, which is a beautiful thing but a total surprise, to me. So we all decided to walked around near the hotel. The morning brought the most beautiful sunlight, peeking through the cracks of the shaded windows that gave off the most amazing energy. It was time to get downstairs, to find that the shuttle was on time and I couldn't wait to get going. I noticed that Trish was getting along well with everyone as I had hoped. It was a good feeling knowing that God helped me navigate these people here and they all seem so happy, except Tripp. Finally! We are boarding the Allure of the seas, I can see the excitement on everyone's face as they walk their way to the ship. Ava, who is a long time friend of Tripp's, ask me; will we be able to go to our rooms to put our bags away, when we get on board. No, not until everyone gets on the ship and they have the emergency drill; I answered. Until then we can walk around and get the lay of the ship; I added.

We were finally allowed to go to our rooms to put our things away. It was a pleasure to find our cabin steward still there, cleaning. I ask if he could please separate the king bed that was in the suite to make two twin beds instead; he happily agreed. As I began to put my things in the closet, I heard the door close behind me. When I turned to look, Trish had left the room. I came down to the promenade deck, to look for them. I found them all at a small pizzeria restaurant having cocktails while eating pizza. I ignored the feeling that I had and sit down. I began a conversation, reminding them that they had to put money on their sea pass cards, in order to use them on the ship for any future purchases, as I pointed towards customer service. No one said anything, so I began to speak again. You guys want to walk around before we shove off; I ask. The party will be on the tenth floor and we have a little time before that happens; I added. They all seemed to rise at the same time, but Trish sort of moved in slow motion until she was in the standing position. She violently turned towards me and shouted....the best think that you did, was to separate those beds! The anger in her eyes indicated to me, that this couldn't have only been about those beds, there was something bigger brewing inside. In the twenty years that I've know her, we have never had an argument. As a matter of a fact, she and I had never had a disagreement until she moved to Indiana, and this was about my son.

I couldn't move from where I stood, for fear that I would be attacked even further. My focus was on her face, the one that after many years of knowing. As I watched, Donna walk over to calm her down. I turned to see the faces of the rest of the group, to possibly gauge their reactions as too what they've just heard. I then rushed to tell my friend, I didn't mean any harm by separating those beds. It's a practice of mine, unless I'm with a female that I'm going to be "with." She scowled at me, that look let me know, that I may have said the wrong thing. Donna intervened; you guys should have worked your differences out prior to this trip, so that it would not have involved us. She was right, I looked in Trish's direction, in hopes that she would do or say something to let them know that I did try to straighten things out but those things had nothing to do with this. She wouldn't even look at me. I'm done; she said sternly. My mouth was hanging wide open. I didn't see this coming. She turned in the other direction and walked away. But what was crazy to me, was that they all walked with her. I was left standing there alone, embarrassed.

Hearing the foghorn of the ship, released me from what was manifesting inside of me. Still not believing what I just witnessed, I began the process of shoving my emotions down deep where all of the other pain reside. I then turned and headed for the elevator. I stepped off on the tenth floor to see a few hundred people dancing to the music. It was live, there were people dancing in the pools, by the bars, near the railing, some with drinks and some without. I took my time to shuffle my way threw the crowd of people to find my friends. After walking for ten minutes or so, I spotted them near the railing on the other side. As I moved closer, I could see that Trish was laughing and seemingly having a good time with my friends. I came even closer and my heart jumped when I noticed Tripp looking in my direction. Her facial expression went serious, instantly. Using small talk, to start a conversation; hey guys; I said. It's beautiful out her, isn't it?

I noticed that whatever was funny to them, was no longer when I walked up. I stayed with them for twenty five minutes, I'd say. I watched as everyone remained straight faced, with no more laughter. Donna, made the announcement that she needed to get Natasha back to the room to lie down and rest, everyone else followed as well. I stayed for a bit longer, thinking. I walked around for a while and went to the room. When I made it back to the room, I laid across the bed, to catch my breath from a long day of travel. As I turned, in walked Trish. Can we talk; I ask. There's nothing to talk about; she said as she got what she came for, turned and walked out of the door. I was so confused, I didn't want to believe what was running through my mind. When I woke up from a nap, I realized that it was dinner time. I showered and caught the elevator up to the windjammer. This restaurant had everything you would want to eat for breakfast, lunch and dinner, from all cultures. I chose to eat here over the formal restaurant. I walked slowly, looking at the food while looking around for them, as well. Finally, I filled my plate, grabbed a drink and found me a seat near the window, where I could look out at the ocean. When I finished, my curiosity was getting the better of me. So, I searched the places on the ship where I though they might be and sure enough they all were sitting together enjoying themselves. When I noticed that I had been seen, I walked over and sit for a bit and announced that I was going to bed because we port early in the morning. Sadly, I was the only one of us to move. I held my head high and walk away.

I awake at six am, found that Trish was gone already. As I walked out on the balcony, I can't help but admire St. Thomas. It was beautiful this time of year, with the blue waters that lined the beaches, just breathtaking. I hurried to get dressed to go up to the windjammer in hopes of finding them, so that we could possibly walk off the ship, together. I couldn't wait to show them my favorite places on the island. I'd been to St. Thomas twice before on other cruises, "however I was fine coming back, to be with my friends." When I made it up there, they weren't in sight. So I ate my food and made my way towards the gangway, to exit the ship. I looked up to see Ava. I put my camera around my neck and proceed to walk towards her and noticed the rest of them standing a bit to the side, talking amongst themselves. It became obvious to me, that they were waiting for Ava to exit the ship and not me. I came off behind her and caught up with them, where are you guys headed; I ask. Right here; Natasha said, pointing to an area where the natives are selling souvenir's. Lets take a shuttle out to see the town; I suggested, trying to keep my voice from shaking. Well, we didn't plan for that, Tripp said; as she disappeared into the makeshift building. I walked in with them and realized that this wasn't what I wanted to do. I said my goodbyes, walked until I found a place where I could catch a shuttle out, to see more of the town.

My thoughts were all over the place. I had six days left on this cruise and something had to change. I took it upon myself to make that change. When I made it back on the ship, I went to the cabin to find Trish, grabbing things again, to leave the room. Can we please talk; I ask. She walk past me without saying a word and walked out. I sit with my head in my hand, not quite knowing what else to do about our situation. I showered and went up on the 10th floor to eat. To my surprise, they were all together, eating, as well. When I made it close enough, that they could hear me; I called you all earlier, to see if you all wanted to go to the club tonight; I ask. They all agreed, we set a time and a place to meet. Tripp, Ava and Natasha, laughing, admitted that they were going to take a nap, first. We're back to normal, I thought. Fast forward... there was no one at the spot that we agreed upon. They were already, inside of the club, when I made it there. I pushed past the pain that was overwhelmingly consuming me and carried on as if, nothing happened. As the night ended, I didn't see Trish. I assumed that she went to our room early but when I finally made it there, she wasn't there. We were out to sea for an entire day and there were a few things on our itinerary to do for the day and the evening. I made a mental note to self, "stop by customer service after breakfast."

As, I approached customer service, all that I could think about was how bad this could turn out. Hello ma'am, may I help you? The lady behind the counter, ask. Yes, I hope so. My name is Trul'ee Benevolence, I'm in cabin 736, and I would like to know if I could possibly finish out my cruise in another room. Is there anything wrong with the room? She ask. No, there isn't, but I feel that I'm dwelling in a hostile environment and I would like to deescalate the situation in this manner. Although, I haven't been threatened or harmed in anyway, there is a lot of tension. So, if I could be removed, I believe that it would be best for both parties; I added. Well, your in luck, there is a passenger that will debark in the morning at our next port. We will let you know when the room is cleaned for you and we will also, assist with moving you, if you need. Thank you, Thank you so much; I said before walking away.

Tonight's entertainment, was the Ice Capades. I walked in, to find the friends sitting to the left. Natasha was waving for me to come on over, as I made my way closer. The show started and I couldn't hear anything that she was saying, so I signaled that we talk after the show. She seemed so eager to tell me something, during the show but when it ended, she lead me to believe that it wasn't a good time. So, I walked behind them, watching as they all seemed to have conversations with one another. That little man on my shoulder began to talk to me, "you look like a damn fool" it said loudly. But, I knew that I was practicing patience and tolerance among ignorant people. But this required much more tolerance, than I thought.

Again, Trish was gone by 5am. So, after breakfast, I received the call from the front desk. I swiftly made the move to the new room. I looked back on all of the times that I have cruised, I have never had a cabin to myself. This, gave me time to think about, all that has happened. I got my camera and walked off the ship alone to do a little shopping for my grand babies. I saw them just outside on the pier, she must have told them by the looks on their faces. As I walked closer, Tripp spoke first. Man, you left the room? Man, that was low down. Hey man, I want peace. I want her to enjoy her vacation as well as I; I added. You two need to make up; Donna said. But there was no amount of words said, that would sway her too undo what she's done. Everyone began to chime in. I felt as if my character was being ripped apart. The only person who had know me the longest was Trish, twenty years and she was the reason for this confusion. The next, was Natasha, eight years and she didn't come to my defense not once. I felt betrayed by the both of them. I knew at that moment, that I will never, truly trust again.

This was wild to me. I see them in different places on the ship however, I stay my distance. I got off alone at the next port and did my excursions, alone. When I came back on the ship, I was alone however, I had a good time. We are out to sea again. I went to the formal dinning room to eat tonight, they are there at our table. Trish looks beautiful in a dress and makeup, I've never seen her dressed like this before. She's usually in hunting gear, shorts and a t-shirt or camouflage, type clothing. As I sit in silence, I feel a nudge from under the table. I look up to see Natasha's face, she indicates that she wants me to smile. I gave her a half smile and turned away. As I listen, I hear them all say, that they have enjoyed their vacation together. Although none of them, have been or seen anything past port. I'm not sure that they have even explored the ship, fully. They flocked around Trish and hung on to her every word as she shared her many stories about herself. I now know through conversation, that she and Donna were meeting at 5am, to walk every morning before breakfast. I did not want to be there but my pride would not allow me to leave. I wondered why my black friends sided with my white friend. I could only wonder, because my pride wouldn't allow me to ask.

The next day was Jamaica. I ate my breakfast, and exited the ship to see them once again. I was ask by Natasha, where I was going. I don't know; I said. I watched as they walking into a makeshift hut that sold souvenirs, again. I shake my head in disgust, as I walked out to find transportation into town, again. I found a bus, that was beautifully decorated with no windows. I pulled out my camera and took pictures of all of the beauty that surrounded me. When I made it to town. I met a Jamaican woman in a small tent, who says she's 90 years young. She had, many beautiful things to be sold, that she say, were made with her own hands. I went in to see her merchandise. I was surrounded by many beautiful pieces, but there was one that I had to have for myself. It was a long turquoise and white dress with a head set to match. I thank you ma'am, this is beautiful; I said. She insist on holding my hand as she looked into my eyes, she smiles. Everything will be fine; she said. I knew this woman knew nothing about what I was going threw, but through her touch there seemed to be a calm, that came over me. God Bless you; I said, and left. I walk around looking for other beautiful things for my grandchildren until it was time to head back.

This is the last night on the ship, I want to enjoy myself, I thought. So, I go to the club and I dance and drink, not much because I have too be on point for our travels home. By morning, our luggage is already off the ship, and all we have to do is meet up. I wait for them, so that we all can board our shuttle to the airport. Right away, I notice that Trish isn't with them. Where is she? She's gone already; Donna admitted. I tried to keep my facial expression in order, as we loaded onto the shuttle. The trip home was very quiet. Upon arrival at South Bend airport, I grabbed my thing, went to my car and went home. I chose to sever all ties from these people however, they would not let me go as easily. Donna and Natasha broke up. Donna thought that Natasha ran into my arms. Never would I cross the line, no matter how crewel you are to me; I said to Donna. She claimed, to be innocent, as to what happened on the ship. I sit in silence. I believed, that this was Carma calling for them. Finally, after a couple of months, the fire smoldered and I was allowed to live my life without them, all but Natasha. She insisted that she was under strict orders from Donna, not to do this or not to do that. Hmm, followers are dangerous to me; I thought. And so are the company that we keep.

Chapter 7

Forgive my shortcomings

I've always been very well aware of the monster that lurks inside of me. My job everyday is to keep it, in it's slumbered state. One way to do this, is too close the doors on people, who purposefully cause me harm, whether it's emotional or physical. So, I returned to my sisters and brothers in the NA program to heal, from what I endured. Step seven, in the book "It works, how and why" We humbly ask Him to remove our short comings. In my case, there were many, for him to remove, so I ask that he forgive them. My way is not always the best, but it works for me. When I left the meeting, I drive over to the Marriott Hotel. As I walk through, I see someone that I knew from the days when I worked here. I instantly feel pride that I've moved on. I arrive at the room and when the door opens, I see the look of a woman, that's willing and able. I put the black bag down on the floor and allow her to come close to me. Her fragrance is alluring, it makes me want her even more. But I think, that I want to make love to her without the bondage, this time. I proceed, with confidence.

I pull her close. While looking into her eyes, slowly tasting every part of her lips to finally take the time to part them with my tongue. As she allows me in, I explore. I then began too kiss her passionately, admiring her scent which, is driving me wild inside. I can see the confusion in her eyes but she likes what she's feeling so, she allows it. Pulling her robe past her shoulders to allow it to fall to the floor. She whispers; please fuck me, as I kiss along the side of her neck. I put my finger to her lips, urging her to be silent as I continue to touch and admire her body. She's squirming as I touch near her inner thigh, she wants to open them but I gesture, that she not. As I continue to caress her body. I can feel her quiver as I move towards her sweet spot.

Slowly, moving her backwards towards the bed, while kissing her softly. The more that she moans, the more turned on I become. I'm fighting the urge, not to forcefully pull her hair back, to gain more access to her neck and bite as she likes. She finds her spot on the bed, I take my things off and put my thang on, to join her in an attempt to work out all of my aggression. As I mounted her, she let's out a screams. The further in, that I went, she screamed even louder. I'll give you something to holler about bitch; I thought. The harder I pound, the louder she screamed. I apply three fingers to her lips, in an attempt to quiet her but, she continues to scream. I then put my hand up to cover her mouth but she's still screaming. While I'm shoving my shaft inside of her, I slowly put my hands around her neck, as I'm entering her again. I squeeze. I find that this is satisfying to me, so I fuck her even harder, as she's gasping for air. I'm reaching my climax, I feel it! It's my time to scream, Ahhhhh! Oh my God! I then let go. She's able to breath freely now. I see tears streaming down the side of her face. You did a good job baby, I whisper in her ear, as I'm kissing her face and stroking her hair.

She's melting into my arms as I nurse her, back from beyond. I then assist her into the shower. There, I lather her up and clean every area of her body, paying extra attention to her sweet spot. She moans, in an attempt to get my attention. I fondle her until she cum's, oh my God, it's squirting! I have never seen this before. I stay there until she's done, I then look down to see that it's all over my hand. Once, she's cleaned, I oil her body down in hopes to put her to sleep. When I wake in the morning, she's laying there staring at me while I sleep, what's up baby? I ask. That was the best sex that I have ever had; she said with conviction. You know your worth, don't you? she added. I kissed her on the lips, and lightly touched her neck, got up and began to dress. Checkout isn't until 11 am; she said. I have to go, dear. I kissed her once again, turned and grabbed the money on the desk. I made it to the door, blew her a kiss and closed it behind me. I looked down at my hand as I waited for the elevator to see eight hundred dollars, I smiled as I stepped into the elevator.

==

I've secretly harbored resentments for most of my life, for those who had harmed me in my past. I forgive you….I've said in my mind many times, but because I said it, it wasn't so. I've told myself and others that I had forgiven them but because I couldn't forget, there it was, manifesting in ways that I, myself could not control at times. For instance, during my sexual encounters, I had to concentrate more on the task at hand to keep myself from causing harm to those involved. I've added it to my daily prayer of things that I wanted God to remove. I thought about my mother and the pain that she must have had too carry around all of her years. Only because of the way she treated me, I thought. This dreadful cycle of pain must end, with me. There has to be one person in this wicked world that I could trust enough to talk too{other than a shrink}, I thought. Even at my age, people in my life weren't very trustworthy. I have a lot of people that don't like my flava, so to speak. I was told, "if you don't have haters, that means you ain't doing it right." I walk proud, because I know where I came from and by the grace of God, I have no intent on returning.

My children were an inspiration, in spite of all that we have been through, they still excelled. I loved watching, as each one of them spread their wings as they left the nest. I did as most parents did back then, we prepared them for life and when they turned 18, we helped with their transition into adulthood. I'm getting older now, and I wished that I had kept them at home longer. I believe that there are or were some resentments because of my choice to do this. I've had the pleasure of watching my children make their way through life exploring different avenues. But what I loved most, was that I was allowed to be a part of the process. High school, proms, Collage, and then careers, which gave me many proud, mommy moments. Now, it was time for me to find my soulmate. Someone who would except my flaws and be patient, as I learn to love again.

Her name is Salina, she and I had birthdays two days apart. I've known her for years however, I've looked at her, as just a friend.

She, for what ever reason, set her sights on me. She chased me for months and finally, I stopped long enough to have a conversation. Her words seemed to have a sense of urgency, so I stayed to listen further. Smooth, is what I called her. She was a beautiful dark piece of chocolate that melted in my mouth whenever I kissed her. As the months past, she helped to bring me out of myself, just a bit. Everywhere, that she went, she made sure that I knew, and ask that I show up for at least a little while. I would usually make an appearance and on occasion, I would stay a little longer only because, it felt good to be wanted by her. I worked 3rd shift, then. She ask that I stop by for a kiss on the way. There were times that I would show up a little earlier and give her a little more than a kiss. She never knew about the other side of me only because, she didn't ask. Although, if she had....

She's good people, but I had an issue with her yesterday. When we'd go out on a date, she would invite him. He was a mutual friend of ours from years back, as well. He's a good man, nice dresser, funny. Usually, I don't mind his presence but if I wanted to take her out on a date, she would invite him to come, as well. I wanted this time with her, alone. When I brought it up, she would be on the defense about it. He's my BFF; she would say. And where I go, he goes. Now, I know that there are women who like hanging out with their gay, guy friends. But, as I said, I have no issues with it any other time but, when I request her time alone for a date, that's what I expect. I found, that she wasn't a fan of public affection either. Now, I wasn't a person to go all out about it but, holding hands and an occasional kiss on the cheek......even when in front of our friends. I couldn't be as understanding of this, as she may have wanted me too.

To me, this was a form of rejection. I had experienced enough of it in my past, to last me a life time. Without her knowing my story, she couldn't have possibly known. However, conversations were had and still, she did as she wished. It happened a few more times and her explanation didn't make me feel any better, so I ended us. I wanted us to return to just being friends but, when she wouldn't answer my calls, not respond my texts, I knew that is wasn't possible. Months later, I was told by a mutual friend of ours, that she was in love with me and that I broke her heart. I wondered, how can a person love what they've rejected time and time again?

Now, it's time for me to learn more about myself. My limitations, my expectations, likes, dislikes and most of all, who I would prefer, to spend my time with. I set reachable goals myself. I learned how too incorporate humility and how to transfer negative energy into a positive. The hardest of them all was, to learn to trust. I'd hoped, that I would learn to do this, one person at a time. This was truly a trigger for me, too the point that I had to talk about it with my sponsor, from time to time. Surprisingly, my journey lead me to the library. Where I felt, that after all of my years of not wanting to read a book, actually was a good thing. This opened up a world that I never knew existed. Now that my life has calmed down, maybe this would be a turning point. The first book that I choose, was "The bluest eyes" by Toni Morrison. I read it trice to get the full context. I then rented another called, Beloved. After reading yet another one of her novels, I would learn that through her writing, I would find some truth about life as a black person in this nation. You know, those things that were happening to us, that weren't added in text books in school. Iyanla Vanzant{Living through the meantime}. Was another book that I chose, as I worked on self healing. Gary Chapman {The five love Languages}. Fredrick Douglass {Prophet of Freedom}. I felt that this book was deep but filtered. I also picked up books by Donald Goines, {Swamp Man} and {Whore Son} and a few others, whom I felt was, by far the best urban writer to me. Iceberg slim, who was the second best. My proverbial mind was all open to this new way of educating myself. After all of these years, I was finally excited about learning.

 I still desired the scent of a woman. It seemed that, attempting to find one in South Bend was far and between. After all of the clubs closed and friends became scarce. There wasn't many places left for us to meet. Of course, there were women who were bi-curious in the straight clubs but the fear of "what others would think of them" outweighed the experience. So, I turned to the internet. It turned out to be a flop. So, my focus became those old friends that left me years ago. I found most of them on Facebook and the others received news that I was looking for them, by word of mouth. A blast from the past is what, I called it. I invited them all to come together at a place called; Franks Place in South Bend. I was very surprised as to how many, showed up. I could tell by all of the love shown, that they all missed each other as well. I was a bit emotional seeing this. We had an amazing time together. Unfortunately, I didn't see or hear from them, for two years after that night. I then, called on them again after two and a half years. I invited them to meet up at an establishment called, Bar Louie. It was as if, the love that was being shown, created a closeness between us the was last a lifetime. Unfortunately, I haven't seen or heard from the majority of them, since. I returned to the journey of learning more about me. I began to travel more, which brought me joy. There wasn't a year that went by, that I wasn't going somewhere new.

 I wanna back track a bit…One night, I walked into a bar by the name, of Dockside. It was now, know to be another gay bar in the area. I came there that night, to get seating arranged for my friends daughter and her bridal party. They all wanted to see the drag show that was taking place that night. As I began to put the tables together, I turned to notice Donna standing there, which surprised the hell out of me. I walked over, and began talking to her, I notice this lady staring at me. I turned back to Donna to ask; what brings you here tonight? As she began to speak, I look around the bar to notice that our entire group of friends, are here. Sadly, I didn't get the memo because, I am the only one of us that would have been missing. {This was an encounter well before the end of our friendship, I missed the warning sign}. I tuned out and didn't hear anything that she said, at that point. However, my friend and the bridal party, walked in. As I guided them all to their seats, I notice that this lady is still staring at me, while licking her lips, this time. Who does that? I ask myself. I smile and return to the bridal party. An hour has passed, and it's my time to go. As I stand to leave, a song is played that I like. I veer over to the dance floor and began to dance. This same lady, boldly comes up to me without words and began dancing with me, while pressing her large breast up against my chest. I turn around to avoid this interaction but she comes around to face me. I smile and began to walk off of the dance floor. She follows me, I wave to my friend and walk towards the exit. Before I made it to the threshold, she calls out for me too stop. I turn, she looks as if winded and says; my name is Lynda and I think that you are a very beautiful woman, I would like to get to know you better. I walked to the bar, wrote down a number, handed it to her with a smile, waved goodbye to the owner of the club, nodded to her and left.

July 2018, was one of the most exciting and lively days that I had experienced in such a long time. I felt, that God had to have a hand in this, after the horrible experience I had on the cruise with my ex-friends. I couldn't close my mouth, due to all of the vibrant signs and billboards that were lit up in the daytime, throughout the ride in. I ask the Uber driver to pull over, so that I could get a picture. The LasVegas sign, had me in awe. As we moved through the city, it was a lot to see. I couldn't wait to get out and be a part of the crowd that I passed while riding. When we pulled up in front of the Stratosphere Hotel, I couldn't wait to get out to see more. I've never been in a place, where there were so many casinos and so much going on at one time. When I made it to the room, it looked average but nice. But, when I walked over to the window. In disbelief, I looked back at Lynda, with a smile as I nod, to let her know that I am pleased. I could see the entire strip and most of the city from where I stood, this was the best room in Vegas to me.

I needed to step out, get a feel of this place. But I found that the heat was something different, something I'd never experienced, almost unbearable. I went back in after going to the dispensary, which was across the street. I made a decision to head out later, when the sun went down. As the dusk of dark approaches, I could see lights shinning in the distance as we walked to the bus stop. When we came closer to our stop, I could feel the butterflies swarming around in my belly, as I watched people walking this way and that. Entertainers performing throughout our walk down Fremont Street was cool to see. Suddenly, I hear people screaming, that caused me to look back and upwards towards the sky, to see two people Zip lining down the middle of the street. Wow! Was all that I could say. I know that she could see the excitement in my face. I chose to do a little shopping in a couple of stores on the side street and decided to go back to the room to get ready for tomorrow.

Freshen up…I said, in a low tone. Twenty minutes later, I no longer hear water running. Soon after, the door opened. The silence in the room seems to make her uneasy by the look on her face. Assume the position; I ordered in a stern tone. I turned to get things in order, while putting on a song from my playlist called, "Riders On The Storm" which, was one of my favorites. I remained still for a few minutes. I turned to face her, she looked ready but apprehensive. However, I tell myself, she'll be alright. Foreplay moistened everything up nicely. I entered her with ease and kept an even pace. Listening to her moaning only intensified each move, made. I came close to her ear; are you ready for the ride? I whispered. Yes; she said. I pulled out of her pussy and went right into her ass hole. The thrust moved her in a way that she had to re-position her self. I could hear her moaning, through clenched teeth, now. I knew then, that, this nine inch dick was doing as it was intended to do. She flinched but took it all in, as if it were traveling down her throat. I remembered something that she said when we met…I'm looking for something different. "Well, say Hello to different" I thought out loud as I stood to my feet to get a straight shot inward. I held on to her outer thighs with my inner thighs and fucked her as hard as my body would allow. I could actually feel the end of her, insides with every thrust. Minutes later, I think I hear something but I'm in too deep…RED!! RED!! she yells out. I can't stop. She yelled; RED! Once more, I stop.

All that was heard was my heavy breathing, throughout the room. I'm too exhausted to pull out right now, so I lay on top for a while and listen to her whimper. Finally, I slowly began to pull out, I can feel her body shaking beneath me. I can also tell that she's crying. I have to get myself together, so that I can care for her. She's sobbing profusely. You did a good job; I say, while caressing her back, still trying to get myself together. I'm proud of you. As she tries to talk through her tear, I continue to praise her. No one has ever made me feel this good sexually; she admits. I say nothing but I'm flattered. I direct her to the shower and then back to bed.

The next day was truly amazing. We ventured off to see a many things along the strip while taking pictures, every step of the way. We went atop of a roof, to a beautiful restaurant called the "Beer

Gardens" which, the name did not do the establishment much justice. It was truly amazing, though. Too look over and onto the strip below was an unbelievable sight. After having lunch, we walked back onto the strip to see the architectural buildings along the way, I was in awe. The night life was even more exciting. We went to the Champagne bar and over to see the Michael Jackson One by Cirque du Soleil, which was the SHIT! We then, up to the top of the Eiffel Tower to watch the fireworks and the water display at the Fountains of Bellagio. The next evening was pretty cool as well. I was like a kid when we went to see the artifacts of the Titanic. I made sure to gamble at least once, just to say that I did, before going home.

Lynda, kept in constant contact, making sure to stay in my head. Holding my attention, to the point that no one else was able to gain it. She didn't have much to say on the phone but her actions spoke volumes. She was a Michigander, and traveling here or anywhere that I was, was nothing to her. She kept her word when it came to me but, there were times when the occasional white lie would peak it's ugly head. I made her aware that this was a red flag to me. I promise that I will work on it; she'd say. I should hope so; I replied. December of 2018, she and I flew into Fort Lauder dale, to take a cruise on the Celebrity cruise ship to Cancun, Cozumel and Haiti. I love cruising but this one was for the more seasoned passengers. I wasn't quite ready to relax this much. Although, a beautiful ship, there wasn't a promenade deck and I didn't like that. She and I began to travel quite a bit after this.

August of 2019, we drove to Cleveland to see the production of The Lion King, which was truly amazing. Three of the kids went with, we took them to see a war submarine, which was pretty amazing. In that same year in November, we flew to London England. With me being a big Harry Potter fan, I was like a kid in a big candy store or shall I say, a country. We caught a train called the Eurostar, from London to Paris, that traveled under water. I was truly amazed, documenting every step of the way. We were loving life. After we made it home, we immediately began planning our next trip. We flew into Rome to cruise out of Civitavecchia, Italy. Took a train from Rome to Naples, Florence, Sorrento. Tuscany, Barcelona Italy.

God was surely blessing. I then, ask her to come, so that I may show her where I've lived, once upon a time. Jamie and his two boys flew in to meet us, in Oceanside California. Which, was truly the best part about being there. I took her to see where I lived, sharing memories, of what once was. She admitted that riding along the cost was pretty amazing. I kissed my son and the babies and she and I, then flew into Florida and went to Universal Studios to see the Harry Potter exhibit. We then, headed to port out, to Haiti, Aruba, Curacao, on a cruise ship through Royal Caribbean. The following year, we flew into Buffalo new York and drove across to Niagara Falls, where Jamie and his wife joined us. And then on to Little Elm Texas, where we drove to out to Dallas Texas to enjoy a wonderful time with my oldest granddaughters and my youngest grandsons. Over the time that I've know her, she has become my best friend. Only because of who she is, that has remained, constant.

==

I can only give of myself, what I can. These words ring true each and every time that I spoke them, to those who requested my heart. I felt, that it wasn't a piece of pecan pie that was freely shared to those who ask for it. I've always shown love and done good by people but, they seem to want more. My heart was off limits to those that I felt, didn't deserve it, and there were many. The types of arrangements that I participated in, weren't for those that were emotionally immature. There were rules to this, you had to lay a foundation going in. Make boundaries know and not allow them to be crossed. Play, but not be played with. And to always keep in mind, that if there is a time that you are no longer able, nor do you want to provide these services, you will see signs, that the profound love, that is claimed to have for you, will wither away, in time. In my opinion, people are expendable. Every woman has her own wants or needs, and if those needs aren't met well, you are no longer needed. However, I have, for as long as I can remember, been in fight or flight mode. So, for my protection and the protection of others, I come with a manual. It states; If you, the buyer are equipped to handle what the seller is offering, then we may proceed.

Chapter 8

Maintaining The Balance

My life became much better when the grandchildren started coming. I wanted grand babies as early as when my boys were in their late teens. Roland, would just laughed at me when I talked about it. But, Jamie, made me aware that, he had a plan for his life and in the order of things, were that kids, would come after a career and then marriage, which I had to respect. Darion and Jeremiah, were still babies in my eyes, so I thought nothing more about them. God later blessed me with eight grand children. However, my son Roland lost his son Deon in a tragic house fire, that left him emotionally wounded. I felt for my son in a way that I never thought that I would have, too. The road to healing was a rocky one for him.

My grandchildren became more of a reason for my existence, every day. I can admit, I somewhat became obsessed with the thought of being in their lives. I just couldn't imagine any of them admitting that they have no memory of me, when I'm gone. "Thinking back" I ask Jamie and Roland {since they were the oldest} if they remembered my mother/ their grandmother? When the answer was no, this was hurtful to me, especially since we lived with her, at one time. Without hesitation, I went into full Granna mode. I was there for birthdays, holidays, school activities and special events, not to mention, graduations. Always, bringing board games, art projects and assisting with whatever, to help in their growth. While, spending as much time with them all, as I possibly could. When I traveled, I made sure to keep them all involved as well, so that we may be in tune. Although there were times, when I felt as if I had to walked on eggshell with my children, in order to keep contact with the grandchildren. During the time when my children were growing up, I've always been a free speaker, being that I was the alpha in our homes. But, this is their home and their children and I had to remain silent about their parenting skills, not saying that they were bad, just different. I remember; Jamie Jr. buying a baby book when his first son was born. It broke my heart, only because I felt that I would be his go too, when there were questions about my grandson. I also felt as if, maybe this was his way of saying that my parenting wasn't the best in his eyes. As my grandson grew, things were much better. I would see and hear some of my parenting, through my son and this made me very happy.

Communication was the key. Finding new ways to convey my feelings to my children was important to me, hell, they were important to me. Although, I made a few fumbles, I recovered and made touchdowns, so to speak. But as time passed, I didn't realize that I was loosing my younger son Darion. It was happening in plain sight. He has a smile that was as beautiful as the sunrise, with skin dark and smooth as chocolate, with a personality that love had to be made of. But in silence, he was planning his departure. Our conversations in person, were as they had always been but, the difference was in our communications on the phone. There were times that he wouldn't answer at all. And when he'd finally call or text me back, he would always say that he was busy. Not to mention all of the times that I was sent to voicemail. Towards the end, it would take a day or so for him to respond to a simple text. It finally stuck in my head, that something was wrong. However, I didn't stop trying. I'd find myself sitting in heavy thought thinking back, wondering, what could I have done to deserve this. But all that comes to mind, is that he got the best of me. He grew up without the addiction and was a part of the recovery process. It seemed as if he received more of me, than the other boys did. To the point that they thought, that I may have loved him more. I did not, I loved them all the same, it's just that they all required different things from me. "He was the baby" was my defense.

He stayed with his father longer than his brother Jamie did back then. I assumed that maybe his father got into his head during that time, but I then, thought, Naah! He's to old for that shit, now. So…. What could it be? I wondered. It went on like this until he decided to move his business to Atlanta to further his dream. It wasn't long after, that all contact ceased. My heart shattered. I wished that I could say that my kids made it through all of the trauma that I suffered, unscathed. My son Jamie became distant as well, during that time. However, it wasn't in the way that Dorian did but, it was present and when I ask; what's going on? I'm good ma; was his response. And like the domino affect, Roland fell right into place. I felt pain from all areas of my body, it seemed. I allowed the stress to manifest in a way that I became ill, and had to be hospitalized for two days. This was between me, God and the staff at Memorial Hospital. I didn't tell my boys because, I didn't want it to seem as if I were using this as a ploy to bring them back to me. At one time, I felt as if I was being punished for everything that I had done in my past, (Karma). These feelings came about because of all of the love that they showered on their father. Birthday parties, fathers day celebrations and so forth. I tried hard not to seem jealous or envious about it. But it was happening too frequently. I had to ask one day. Why him and not me? Ma, you have many people in your life, he has nobody; Jamie admitted. And then…. Jamie Sr. died. It was horrible to see my aggressor of all of those years, laid out like that. It took a toll on me as well. I lost it for a moment. While choosing to be there for my children as any mother would, at least as much as they would allow. As time pasted, Jamie and Roland slowly began to come back around. Darion, I wondered if he had been gone too long. My love for him never wavered because, this was an unconditional deal for me.

In January of 2020, I took a drive to Kalamazoo Michigan to visit Lynda. She and I had made plans earlier in the month, to ride to Canada by way of Detroit. We finally made it through the Canadian check point. We checked into the hotel and made it to our room. As I walked through this beautifully decorated room, I couldn't help notice how incredibly large the window pane was. But as I stand in front of it, I was amazed at what I saw. There, right in front of me, was Detroit. It was truly amazing to see how God, separated two countries by just a body of water. I had never seen this before, so it took me a moment to tear myself away. I took in a deep breath and finally walked in, to find her. She, had a surprise for me; she said. It required that we be dressed and out of the hotel by a certain time.

Driving thru a long tunnel to come out on the American side, was pretty cool. Once we were out, it wasn't a long drive to where we were going. When we made it to the vicinity of our destination. I had to drive around the block a few times to find a parking space. The fourth time around, I could see more and more black people walking in the same direction, which made me smile. I didn't know what we were going to see but I knew that it was all about me, which hyped me up. Finally, I found a park, we got out and joined a crowed of people walking. As we turned the corner, I could see a large building with it's marquee lit up in the distance. As we walked, I was still too far away to make out, what was on it.

I'm close enough now that I see what's written. "The Spinners" and "The Whispers" in concert at the FOX THEATER. I almost jumped out of my shoes. I kept my cool, though. Our eyes met, she had a big smile on her face, I tilted my head in her direction and kissed her on the cheek. You did good girl; I whispered. As we stood outside, in a line that wrapped around the corner, I could hear what sounds like someone beating on pots and pans but it sounded really good. Finally, getting closer to the building, there is a young man, sitting on a crate playing the hell out of several pots and pans that were strategically placed on the ground, he was jammin. Finally, close enough to peek in, I saw that it was jam packed. Conversations were being had all around me. Once, I made my way through, I was in awe. It was a truly magnificent work of art through out this place. Everywhere I looked, I was impressed. I finally found where I could get popcorn and a beverage. I turned to walk up a flight of stairs to see yet more beauty about this place. We walked in to what I thought was the auditorium but this was truly an art exhibit to me. I moved to the side to allow others to pass, so that I could look up to the ceiling to admire the artwork. It was unlike anything that I had ever seen. I got my shit together, turned to follow her and the person leading her to our seats, only to see that we are in the second row from the stage. I was blown away! I kept my cool as I reached over to give her yet another kiss. As the music began, I turned to look behind me to see a sea of black and white people throughout. I saw more folk here, than I have ever seen in one place at one time, in my life. I could feel my heart rev up with excitement.

Dam, that was a good show; I said out loud. I have only been to one other concert before, I admitted. And that was Anita Baker, and when I saw her, I cried. Only because, when time were rough back in the days, her music was what I had, to bring me through. Thank you. She looked at me, I watched as her smile grew larger. Now, time to make our way back to Canada; she said, with a sense of pride about her. I noticed on the way back, she took me over a large bridge this time, if I had to guess, it would have been for change of scenery. It was nice. Walking into the lobby of the hotel, I was still excited, talking about what I had just seen. This brought attention to us as they responded with smiles. Finally, making our way to our room, I looked forward, to see that the window was still open from earlier in the day. I walked towards it to be amazed. My God; this is amazing; I whispered. All of Detroit was lit up, with the GM building sitting near the water. As I look slightly to the left I see the Canadian flag, flying high. Picture perfect, in the night. I pulled myself away from the amazing sight and turned to face her; go and freshen up, I said with urgency. She deserved what I was about to put on her.

The next morning, we hit the mall in Canada, where I brought a my first pair of $150.00 pair of shoes. I realized that I have developed a serious shoe fetish. We hung out a bit, had lunch, walked over to the casino, played on a machine, just for the sake of saying that we played and returned to our room to prepare for our ride home in the morning. This was a very nice mini vacation. As we ride up to Lynda's apartment building, I felt an overwhelming amount of gratitude. I park, turn to hug her tight. My ride home was calming. I put on some gospel, and brought it on in. Upon arriving into South Bend. I chose not to go home, instead I went to see my grandchildren, to show off my incredible shoes to the girls. As soon as I came in the door, I was giving out hugs and kisses to everybody, as usual. I stayed to visit with my youngest grandchildren, said my goodbyes and made my way around the corner, to my home. Home feels good when you've been away from it. I got in the shower, put on my pajamas and got in bed to watch a little television. I fell asleep on movie and when I awake again, it was the next day. I couldn't move, my legs and arms felt like led. I knew that if I didn't get up I would urinate on myself. So I tried to lift my head, it felt heavy as well. I called my job, I can't come in tonight because I'm not feeling well; I said and hung up. I wondered what the hell was going on with me, was I dying? Day two, was even worse. I simultaneously felt hot and cold. Lynda called but I couldn't speak because my voice was raspy and I was too weak. I promised that I would show signs of life by texting at least, a letter. When I hung up from her, I pushed myself to get up to get the thermometer. I had a fever of 103, I dragged myself to the kitchen to get a large cup of water, I drank and went back to bed with my cup. Day four, I text the letter "L" I could hardly swallow, I was disoriented and still very lethargic. My head was spinning and I felt as if I was not going to make it. I had a mental conversation with God about my situation and on the day five, I was feeling sweaty as if the storm was calming down. Day seven, I text "alive" still not wanting to talk. I was sweating profusely. The juice and soup that had been delivered to the door by another friend was much needed. I slowly made my way to retrieve it, prepared the soup grabbed crackers and went back to the bed.

Ass the storm passed through my badly battered body. I was able to finally sit up without feeling as dizzy or walk without feeling as tired. I turned on the television, the news informed me right away, that there was some sort of a virus that started in Wuhan China that made it's way clear over to the United States. No, way; I said out loud. This prompt me to educate myself even further through the web. I read that, they found a case in Detroit a day or so before we got there, I was floored. I have been off work for two weeks now, feeling like death, over something that originated all the way in china. I read that the US government was shutting down the whole country because of it. I guess they forgot to inform my job because we had to work. When I returned to work, I was hopeful that I would be one of those chosen to take a layoff that was offered due to this COVID. Only because they were offering six hundred dollars for unemployment. I was still feeling the affects of the virus also, so I wanted to be home. That wasn't the case for five of us per plant, only because we were called essential workers. And this, was only because we made a few parts for hospital bed. I was not happy but later, we found out that there were so many on unemployment in the country, that most didn't get their money for months down the line. And, there were those who hadn't had a job in for ever, found a way to file and get it, which caused an even bigger problem. I digress.

There were many businesses being closed down in our community. The fear was understandable, this was huge. As time passed, I had a mask made for every color that I wore, making sure to keep in fashion{vain}. When, there seemed to be no where to go and nothing left to do. I went into my closet and into my safe and pulled out an old manuscript that I had written back in 2008. I scanned through it, smiling as I looked through the pictures and the inscriptions incorporated within. I then decided to re-write, what was already written. Thinking back on how this all began. I could remember wanting all of the pain, frustration and doubt to go away. It seemed to ease those feelings of despair, in the beginning. But as the writing persist, there was a feeling of walking through tethered roses, as the thorns tore through too my soul, to expose my true self. I prayed that God touches my hearts, that guides my hand, to write what is true and factual and with that, I began too tell my story. I then told myself, that I ain't taking nothing to the grave.

Two months had passed. Most of those, that were laid off, came back to work. Almost immediately after, the job posted that there would be overtime. I was angry as hell because I hate, overtime. As the days moved into months of doing 12 hour shifts, Monday thru Friday, my anger heightened. My thoughts of the outside world became a mystery. My days seemed to consume of nothing but going home to cook, write, shower and to bed, to get up and do it all over again. Soon, we were mandated to work on Saturdays as well, this was madness. This went on for what seemed like forever. I watched as people that I had known for twenty years give up their years of seniority and quit or take an early retirement. I thought about finding another job, myself. I ask God for strength to continued on. Working all of those hours made it hard to concentrate on the book but once I saw the first sentence written, I had to continue until completion. Everywhere I went, I brought my computer along to write. My visits to Texas to see my grandchildren, in the airports, vacations, library, sitting in the parks, my job, wherever I found a sense of peace to write, this is what I did, remembering that God isn't done with me yet……………...

When I came too. I could feel something hard, invading my throat that protrude out between my lips. It was large enough to prevent me from speaking. There was a loud humming noise coming from the right of me that got my attention. I couldn't believe as to how large this machine was. I followed the hoses that ran from my mouth to this monstrosity, finally realizing that it was attached to me. July sixteenth 2022, is the day that I will never forget. This was the day that my body betrayed me. My brain somehow told my lungs to stop breathing. I wanted to cry out, but I first needed to have a reason. I began to point, letting the nurses know that I needed something to write with, because Lynda couldn't quite figure out what I was indicating. Once I attained a pencil and paper there was no stopping me. As, I wrote, I looked over and thought; some genius invented a machine that pushed air into those who couldn't breath for themselves. I've heard stories about it, but had never seen one before, oh how grateful I was at that moment. One hour later, I was allowed to breath and talk on my own, I did so with ease however my inner self demanded to be let loose. Upon release from the hospital, I took the time to look over the instructions that were given to me. It said, that I am to follow up with a neurosurgeon, so that he/she can explain what's going on inside my brain.

Fast forward...I have something called; a Cavernous Malformation. The Dr. explained, I can live with this with monitoring but this is something that I have to deal with for the rest of my life. And that, I do. I have headaches from time to time, nothing major. It feels as if, it travels down through my spine because of where it is, in my head. There are those, who have this thing worse than I, for them, I pray. Something inside of me, was stuck on repeat and continued to ring in my head. Life is too short, it's much too short, over and over again. I was afraid that this thing would happen again, in the same horrific way and take me out for good. I remembered when my mother died and how much of me, I felt that she took with her, that left me empty and hopeless. I also remember how much doubt, confusion and feelings of abandonment, that she left with me as well. I made a conscious decision, that I will not leave my children in this state. I got back to writing again, this incident became my true motivation.

I wrote my way through the COVID, regardless as to how tired I was from working the twelve hour shifts. Halfway through, I thought about those many pages of poetry that I had written and had stored away from back in the year, 1990 and on. I took the time to get those together. I also ask that my family and friends contribute a poem of their own and I published yet another book. Once that was finished, I continued writing. The fear that came over me was immense, only because I was sharing the most intimate parts of my life. I then thought, maybe, just maybe, there is someone in this world who needs to read this story in hopes that it will help them. So, I continued on. The closer that I came to finishing, "Changes Not Seen/ Were Hidden In Plain Sight" My anxiety level had reached an all time high. I stopped, took a break, to just reflect. During the break, all that I kept thinking about were memories. Memories that my children, recalled not having of my mother, and their encounter with her during their young lives. Memories that I wanted my grandchildren to have of me. I began to write one more book, with conviction. I started putting the pages together, writing one word after another, attempting to explain what my heart felt for them, before these babies were even born and how I have incorporated them into my life, today.

I searched and searched, to finally find an Illustrator. When I explained my vision, he understood and helped me bring it to life. This brought on a three and a half month, long relationship with a very kind and patient human being. Lynda and I were in Universal Studios in Orlando Florida, when I received the final draft of the illustrations that were to go into the book, I was overly excited. I went on line, purchased a bar-code and published a children's book on Amazon, myself. This book came into fruition with love and dedication. I got back to writing my memoir, to finally, finish. "Changes Not Seen"... and published it on my own, as well.
I took a small break. To take a look at what I had accomplished thus far. I was on overload. To remember and relive, each and every traumatic experience that I had gone through, took a tole on me, so, yea, this was a much needed break. One month had passed. I got back on the horse (writing) to start the second part of "Changes Not Seen." One word after another, it came to life. This book seemed to

have girth, the content was more intense, more sound. As I write, it dawned on me, "I never thought that I would be sitting her, telling my story."

As the days turn to weeks, I felt that I needed to incorporate something that brought me joy, to balance things out. So I picked up a hobby of building Lego's, not just any Lego's, these were of places that I have gone in the States and in Europe. I started building the Cathedral of Notre Dame de Paris. Between work and writing, this put me in a healthy mental space. But then, there are those days that my mind shifts. It wonders into the dark spaces that are left unattended by the gatekeepers in my mind. I can vaguely make out what's there, I know from past experience that I shouldn't go in, so I don't. If only others knew about the war that goes on from within, the war between good and evil, they would surely think that I'm crazy. But crazy, I'm not. I fight, to be a better person than I was the day before.

I assumed she noticed my hesitation, are you OK? She ask. I lift my eyes from the spot on the rug, that gathered my attention. Without words, I slowly walked towards the partition that separated the sleeping area from the rest of the room. I poured myself a shot and drank it. After repeating it three more times, I told myself that I was ready now. I then moved closer to the bed and knelt down near her ear. Remain quiet; I whispered as I placed all five of my nails into her skin. As I dragged my nails from her shoulders to the tip of her ass, I watched while the track marks grew darker across her body. I could see her anticipation by the way she attempted to follow me, listening, trying to find my whereabouts. I noticed her shivering as I moved silently, yet trying not to startle her. I quietly picked up the flogger and began to massage it, in my right hand.

While making an S shape across her backside, I watched as she reacted to the feel of it. I then spanked her lightly on both cheeks. She spread her legs exposing her clitoris. I swung the flogger swiftly and watched as it landed in the crack of her ass which made her jump. She did as instructed and didn't make a sound. I smacked her again and again and watched as the welts formed all across her backside. I took a moment, not feeling fully focused. I reached on the table and quickly pulled the titty clips and held them in my hands. I instructed her to hold still as I opened one and placed it on her left nipple, as it hung beneath her. I watched her squirm as I opened up the other one and put it on the right nipple immediately after. She yelled out, as I tugged at the chain that connected them both. I don't want to hear you again; I said. Yes, Mistress! She shouted. I pulled at them, to make sure that they were secure, and walked away. When I returned, I moved close to her. I notice that she's shivering again but I say nothing. I slowly take my finger and move around the opening of her anus, applying pressure. I added lube and I watched her, as I moved inwards. Adding yet another finger, the a third as I slide all three, inside of her. I can tell that she loves what I'm doing to her, as I move in a circular motion. I then add a fourth finger and then my thumb. She's open now, more relaxed; I thought to myself. I took a bit of lube and added it to the opening of her vagina with my other hand and watched as she seem to come alive even more. I slowly put the tip of my 9inch dick into her pussy. I began to gyrate, moving at a snails pace. Making sure to touch bump her walls inside. When the moment felt right, I picked up the pace. I reached over and picked up an extra large steel ball and carefully pushed it into her anus. I pushed until the entire ball was inside of her. I hear her moaning but this isn't enough for me, so I pick up the pace and fuck her fiercely. I pound until I know, she feels me.

Thirty minutes later, I can tell by the way she's moving that she wants more but I'm tired, so I stop. I stand behind her to catch my breath. I then pull out and stand quietly listening to the jazz that's playing in the background. I then began to play inside of her with my fingers as if, playing a string a quartet. I then reach for the other ball and slowly push it inside of her vagina, I hear her moan again. When I feel as if I've gotten a second wind. I place the tip of the dick at the entrance of her vagina, moving it around in a circular motion, which seems to stimulate her. I slowly pushed in and out, in and out, until I feel like doing something different. I could feel the resistance inside of her but the pressure that I feel against my pelvic bone is stimulating me as well. I wanted to feel more. I stood on the tips of my toes and slammed the penis into her, over and over and over again. I hear her, but it's not the safe word. So, I give her what she's wanted the entire time I've known her. All rational was gone, the alcohol had taken control. I pushed that dick in and out to the point that I could no longer see the shaft anymore.

After I hear the safe word being shouted in the air, I began to slow my rhythm while caressing her backside. While, telling her how proud I am of her. She moaned, and then began to sob loudly. I pulled out slowly and ordered her to stay in this position as I walked into the restroom to get a towel with soap and water to clean those precious parts of her body. The coolness of the towel seems to soothe her. When done, I ordered her to lay down and I laid beside her. Speaking softly while caressing her backside, reminding her as to how incredibly strong I believed her to be. Putting great emphasis on how proud I am of her for taking what I just put on her. I then lay silently touching her body, as the music filled the room, to bring her back from that place, beyond.

I put two of my fingers inside of her vagina. I slowly, move them around, in an attempt to break the suction that the steal ball has created. She's moaning, not knowing what's going on. I can't get it out! I shouted in my head, while pulling and probing inside of her. I can't get my fingers deep enough inside to loosen the grip that her body has formed around this ball. She's calm, but I'm beginning to worry that we may have to take a trip to the ER. Does it hurt? I ask; No; she says calmly. Does it feel uncomfortable? No, she repeats. This woman trusted me with the care of her body and sadly, I've mishandled her. I decided to wait in hopes that her body pushes it out, on it's own. I can feel that it's moved, she says, with a look of pride on her face. She laid on her back, spread her legs, as I went inside of her and retrieved the large ball. Relieved, that I hadn't hurt her, my immediate thoughts veered towards never doing this again. Although, this is and always has been requested of me. I now feel that the way we choose to practice, has run its course.

Chapter 9

Alone in my joy

Tell me about Tru? She ask with a straight face. My attention shifted towards the floor, as I tiptoed through my memories, to see what was safe to share about myself, again. I've seen this woman many times throughout my adult life, never has this question been ask of me. I've always taken the conversation in the direction in which I wanted it to go. After a long pause; I have a soft spot in my heart for children. Why? she ask. I took a moment to think, while wrenching my hands together in my lap. Being a child was a frightening and unpredictable time in my life. To think of another child having to spend any amount of time in that same space, in unacceptable to me; I said. No child should have to feel like that, so if I can help, I will; I added.

If your children were sitting here right now, how would they describe their lives growing up with you? She ask, while sitting back in her chair, as if to be proud of herself for asking. I wanted to get up and walk out on her ass. But I then, realized, she was definitely earning her money today. I shuffled around in my chair, which was positioned with it's back to the window. Can I move this chair? I ask. I turned the chair slightly, so that I can see the sky. When I returned to face her, I see a slight smile on her lips that brought on a smile from mine, as well. I went up into the attic of my brain, stomping around trying to find an endearing memory to share with my therapist about my boys.

As I began to speak, I wondered why would I start this conversation defending myself? I wasn't a perfect parent, I admitted. But I did the best that I could, with what knowledge, I had. First off, I believe, that my children would admit that their mom is cool to any adult, that ask. But their friends, would receive a warning. Because, I was that parent that would drill them. I needed to know who my children were affiliated with. I wanted to know who their parents were, their siblings, where their kin folk grew up and so on. And if I wasn't satisfied with the answer, they weren't allowed in my home. Soon after, there would be conversations had with my children, about said child. I knew at an early age, that the parent is the first line of defense. In spite of all of the trauma that I had endure as a child, I swore that I would share as much time, love and patience with my children, as I possibly could. And with raising black men in these times, I felt that I had to govern them with an iron fist. I see the shock in her face, finally a bang for my buck, I thought. I've never shared anything about my mother nor the trauma that I experienced, as a child. I definitely wouldn't touch on my peculiar sex habits. I didn't feel as if I could trust her with all of that. For the most part, my children seemed to be in a happy place once I left their father and the drugs alone; I added. They played like normal children. I watched and participated in their growth. They played sports like any other child. I'm very well aware, that there was a possibility that my children had their own trauma, from what they witnessed between their father and I. However, I was hoping to create a safe space where we all could talk about it, and heal together. But you didn't; she added, with a straight face. How do you know? I said. I remained silent for what seemed like several minutes, took in a breath and realized that my time with her, had ended. Only because, she had no clue what it felt like, to grow up black. I had come a long way and it showed in the conversations that we were having. Either, she wasn't paying attention or didn't cares. But, in the back of my mind there was a fear, a fear that without her, life for me would surely crumble and I would have absolutely no one trustworthy to talk, too. I didn't know her, nor did she know those people that I knew, so I felt safe sharing what little, I shared with her. The faith that I worked so hard to build, tends to waiver at times. And yet, I knew that I had to step away from her, in hopes of rebuilding that faith.

Years had gone by without any real thought of getting high. I told myself, without dwelling on it, I would remember some of those horrible things that happened back then, in hopes that I not return. When I think of the fact, that I could have shot and killed a man due to my delusional thinking while on that shit, should be the one thought that keeps me clean. Living in a world that is now beyond cruel, I had too find different ways of coping to eliminate this exasperating fear that I harvest inside.

I can't help but remember, being locked down during the pandemic and feeling that it was somewhat of a joy, a curse or a cruel joke. Sure, there were some that received relief from their jobs and was able to catch up on things around the house. All this, to feel productive but after a while that became monotonous. But, there was a struggle going on inside of me, that put me back into fight or flight mode. During this time, we all saw things on social media and the news, that we can't possibly unsee. I was naive, for thinking that the United States government would come to their rescue, our rescue, these were my people being killed in broad daylight. Sad to say, I prayed for those harmed and their families but I also prayed that it doesn't happen to me or mine. It all took a tole on my psyche, all the same. Since the lock down there were people that I've know for some time now, that have somewhat changed. And there are those, that I just don't trust anymore, due too something they've done or said in regards to me or people my color, lately. Intuitions are heightened now, to the point that I pay more attention to how people move and then, I move accordingly. I want to blame most of their behaviors on what's happened in the world during and after the pandemic. But my personal opinion; I don't believe, that there was one person that made it through this horrible thing, unscathed.

I've learned how to exist without the inclusion of people a long time ago. But, this was the worst that I've known it to be in my lifetime. There are those who chose to stay in my life during this madness that had ulterior motives. I was aware of those motives and chose to ignore them, for the sake of having a friends. There were only a select few who have proven to be genuine. But as I reflect back on some shit, I've also learned to exist without feelings of loneliness which is a "trait" that I've mastered over the course of years, which kept me in a safe, place of peace. It's been said, that everything that you've gone through, prepared you for the things that your going through. I believe this but why should we.

As the quiet storm raged inside of me, I've ask God, on a continuous basis to restore my faith and add a bit of humility, everyday. It wasn't easy for this child of incest to maneuver her way through this life without the armor of God and the twelve step program. There were times, an idea or two would cross my mind that wasn't quite right and because I had been around those tables enough, it seemed to help detour those thoughts that would have otherwise landed me in some shit. And then, to test my faith, my sister Denise dies on March 2017 from complications of lupus. One year later, my little brother Alfred dies February 2018 of lung cancer. I digress. Life has never been easy, but it has been worth living. While being alone in my joy, I have found a way to do this, to the best of my ability.

Chapter 10

In Spite Of

I've witnessed a many miracles as an adult. Most were my own. It has been said, that I am a living testimony as too how good Gods grace, truly is. Too explain…For the most part, my children and I are living, we're healthy and happy, in spite of our past. I've been clean from drugs now for 24 years. Twenty three of those years were spent at the job that I am currently working. I'm a homeowner, that has brought and sold one home, to buy another. I have four children whom have grown to make me very proud in the lifestyles that they have chosen. I'm also following the progress of some of my foster children's lives through social media and from time to time, I pay them a visit. On occasion, I have invited them on a mini vacation or two. I feed the homeless during the holidays and on occasion during the year, which is something that I plan to improve on. I pay homage to the Hope Rescue Ministries, when ever possible for giving, both me and my son Roland, a place to stay when we needed. I'm grateful for the path that we have chosen.

Remembering, those darkest moments, that were spent away from my children when they were young. Sitting in a jail cell for six months, not being able to see them, nor talk to them for five of those months. While in there, I wrote a lullaby for my boys and thirty years later, in December of 2023. Jamie Jr. thought enough of it, to purchase studio time, so that I could go in to record, Rock-A-Bye- Babies. Which was truly amazing to me. I am now an author, {which I find hard to admit} who has written almost five books. I've also been told that my smile is very contagious and it lights up a room. Only God knows how long it took me, to get here. Being told all of my childhood that I was ugly and spending most of my adulthood, believing it. I have been told by the most wonderful children that I know, that I am, the best Granna in the world, which is pretty damn special to me. I've never proclaimed to be perfect but I strive for perfection in the things that I do. I walk with my head towards the sky, thanking my father with each step that I take. I move with confidence, and exercise humility on a daily basis but grant you, I am a work in progress. Trying to channel the negative energy into a positive, yet realizing that some days are harder than others, was quite a task for me.

 I'm blessed to finally have a friend in my life, who has shown me what being genuine means. From the very beginning, I've know what our relationship would consist of, only because she made it perfectly clear as to what and how she wanted it. Her desires for me were a little short of innocent but made crystal clear, at the time. Little did she know, I understood the assignment and would carry it out, each and every time. After six years, Lynda has never strayed from her primary purpose, and that was, to make me happy. It was a quid pro quo, type of situation. Although, every now and then, the proverbial white lie would peak it's ugly head, that would create a misunderstanding. Although annoying, she would make it right. I appreciate this trait in her. Consistency, means everything to me, to the point that I now see her as family.

Although, I have found family in friends with others, some seemed a bit one sided. I felt, I was the only one who was interested in maintain those friendships/family ships. So from those, after years of struggling with the thought of being without them in my life, I've finally detached. There has been a lot going on around me but I've learned to step away from those people, places and things, that had taken away from my serenity. I am alone in my peace now, and have become a better person because of it. And when I say peace, I mean this in ever since of the word. Coming in from the job, I greet my puppy, send her out to the yard to do her business. I put on some smooth jazz, pour a glass of red wine, walk through the house to the bathroom, turn on the shower and bathe. When I'm finished, I go to the kitchen to wash up and began to prep my dinner. Soon, I'm able to sit down to write. I may look outside to check on the dog, but soon after that, she and I are off to bed with a good book. I have no one to answer too but God, and for that I am truly grateful. My life seems to have more balance.

"I know what you need from me but I can only give of myself what I can" This came about only because, there was something that I felt in my spirit, that told me that my heart wouldn't be safe with this person. Of course, their rebuttal has been, that I'm like this because of Yvette. They feel as if the pain has lingered on after all of these years. It's quite the opposite, the pain has since gone but the love lingers on, as friends of course; I answered. I allow them to think what they wish. Little do they know, my guarded behaviors came about in spite of her.

Since I've known you, I've seen how you show love and do good by people and that's what I love most about you, she uttered through gritted teeth. Allowing her words to linger, as I squeezed her nipples with my finger tips. I released them and then squeezed a bit harder and watched as she winced. I then released them again and demanded silence. I waited as moments pass to hear the sound of the house settling near the front of the house. I thought about how I once felt, that this house belonged to the trees that surround it. The amount of respect that I felt for mother nature because of it. She spoke {hard headed ass, I thought}. She's drunk! I knew that the vodka wouldn't take long, it's the antidote that counteracts the courage. She's asking for something that we have never done before. I pondered over it and thought not. She's getting older; thinking to myself. Although I'm older than she is, it's apparent that we are aging differently. Without words, I claw my fingers and watch as she anticipates the pain. I press my nails against her skin and pull them slowly down the side of her body, looking back to see the beautiful masterpiece being created. I lift my nails to reposition them to drag them yet again towards the center of her back. As I make it to the other side of the bed, I smack her ass hard and claw my fingers once again to repeat the process. I watch as her body relaxes. I walk to the foot of the bed to position myself behind her. OK google, I shout in the air. Play Carlos Santana! Black magic woman begins playing from the speaker. I take in all of the instruments that I hear. Reaching down in from of me to grab a hand full of her hair and aggressively pull it into my fist. I reach down with my other hand and grab the tip of my dick, to position it at the opening of her ass hole. I slowly push it inside of her until it stops. I hear her scream out. Shush, I command. She does as she's told. I push with much more force, I hear her whimpering. Shush, I command again. I push her buttocks down to get a better aim and rise up on the tips of my toes as far as I can and ram the dick inside of her as hard as I believe that she wants. I continue to pump harder and harder, with aggression. Gyrating, trying to wake up what ever is sleeping inside of her. I can feel the pain in my calf, it's burning but I don't stop. I pull her hair harder and then let it fall from my hand. I reach around to the front of her neck to grip it. Holding on as I moved inside of her. I then grip her neck tighter, as I fuck her harder. I hear her moaning louder but she's gasping in between but I don't stop because I want her to remember this. I've decided this won't happen again. I continue to fuck her until her legs begin to collapse. I pause, tell her to get back into position and when she does…... I continue to fuck her even harder until... RED!! RED!! She yells. I then stop.

I'm so proud of you. Now lye down, I softly tell her. Once she's on her belly, she begins to cry. I hold her close to tell her that it's over and that she did an amazing job. We lay in silence, as I caress her backside. I finally break the silence, telling her; I don't want to hurt you anymore. She looks at me, as if in disbelief. Why? she ask. We aren't in the best of health to be doing this any longer. I need change. She looked at me as if she's not quite satisfied with the answer and said, OK. But, now I worry that you will leave me; she added. You don't have to worry about that dear. Are you OK to get up now? I ask. Go and shower; I added. She and I remain the best of friends, till this day. We travel and hang out. When at all possible. I won't disappoint people who genuinely care and love me in spite of being me.

As time passed, I ask God yet again, is this it? Is there anything more that you ask of me. With the holidays slowly approaching, I felt a small wave of sadness come over me. Remembering the family gatherings that were had at my homes through out the years. My children, sisters, brothers, sister-in-law all five of her children, friends of mine, friends of my children, as well as my new daughter Elise, who married Jamie Jr. And as they grew to have their own, there were the babies as well. Everyone that came to my home on Christmas had a gift there waiting for them and for those that were unexpected, received something from the extras, pile or money. Those were the days. Memories of when my children became men raced through my mind as well. They made me aware that year, that they were going to spend the first part of the holidays with their grandmother, father and their siblings. Although, I heard them, it took my mind a moment to process what I had just heard. And when it did, I agreed, although it saddened me, still. I felt that this was only the beginning of a much bigger change for us. Turn's out, this arrangement worked out perfect. When they were finished celebrating with their family, they came to me. I had finger foods, chips, drinks, board games, darts, air hockey and the all time favorite, the Wii. We had a ball! This continued on for three years. On the third year, I purchased a home with my family in mind, the middle of the next year, Jamie and his family moved to Texas.
My sister- in- law died on December 2nd of that next year. Soon after, Darion moved to Atlanta. Roland, still resides here however he began to visit his fathers family, on the holidays. The rest of the family dwindled away, doing their own thing as well.

This had me baffled. There wasn't anywhere in this world that I wanted to be but with all of my family, under one roof during the holidays. My heart was broken but because no one ask, I didn't tell. I found that compartment, where I've stuffed all of the pain that I've felt in my life and shoved it deep down inside, where there was no chance of it ever surfacing. Each year after, Jamie made sure that I was a part of the kids Christmas by face time and phone calls as did Roland, until Jamie made reservations for me to be there in Texas with them every Christmas, since. I feel the love when I'm there with them and for that I am truly grateful. While there, I would video chat with the children in South Bend to keep them all connected, in some way.

I fly there often. Jamie has his boys in baseball, soccer and swimming. On occasion, I have flown in, for their games, my granddaughter's graduation from high school and a birthday party. On numerous occasions, the kids have complained that I don't stay long enough. I've explained to them, I come for their special time and I go home, to go to work. My words seems not to reach them, so my son and I conspired a plan for me to stay for two weeks for this up coming Christmas. I arrived on December 21st. My grand dog Lokey was the first to greet me and then all five of my babies came to join in. We had the most amazing time as a family. My son took us all out to dinner and a play afterwards with valet parking. I was truly proud and impressed by how he managed the night. The week after I arrived, I spent the day with my daughter, she and I went thrift shopping, which is something that I love doing. We had a very good time together. A day later my son and I rode to Dallas, on a business venture of his. I saw the most amazing art drawn on the buildings through out the city. We had time to talk, with love filled eyes, I hung on to his every word. I loved the time that I spent with him, it was more precious to me, than he could have ever imagined.

Christmas was beautiful. Everyone had on matching outfits. After opening all of the gifts, my son and I took pictures, of everyone. I played with the boys, with what gifts they had gotten. Watched the girls model off what they had received. We had a good time being family. The next few days were spent getting to know the things about them that I miss, when I'm home. Already dreading the day that I have to leave them. On December 30th my granddaughter decided to do the karaoke thing with me, while my son sit and play his video game. My daughter sit quietly listening to us sing. I decided that I wanted popcorn after I finished my song. "Can't help falling in love with you" by Elvis. Once finished adding my ingredient, I came back to the table where my granddaughter was, to listen to her sing her song. She then passed the mic to her mom in hopes that she would participate.

As she began to sing, I stepped into the dinning room to take a couple of puffs of my inhaler. I turned to walk back into the living room, but noticed that my breathing hadn't improved. So, I returned to the dinning room to take another two puffs. I then turned to walk outside in an attempt to get air into my lungs while feeling the urgency to breath. I opened the door and called for my son. As he turned the corner, I could hear the babies running behind him. I immediately told him to send them upstairs. When he returned to me, I ask; call 911. I can take you ma; he said. No son! Call them! I can feel my lungs began to close up, as my thoughts drifted to my early childhood. "It's funny how in the end your thinking of the beginning. I can feel his body within my hands, I'm holding him as if for dear life. I'm going to die, I whispered to my son as I went down on one knee.

I wake to a familiar sound. As I adjust my eyes, I look around fighting through the blur, to see if the sound is what I think it is. Damn! I'm being intubated again; I screamed, in my head. As my eyes focus even more, I see my son sitting on the couch. I signal for him to come closer. I look down to see that both of my wrists are bound. I'm terrified to know, why. I looked into his eyes, I then looked down and when I noticed that our eyes we focused on my hands, I began to write in the air, he seemed to know what I wanted. Once I received what I needed, I began to put my words to paper. I knew what I wanted to say but I couldn't convey it as of yet, measured by the confused look on my son's face. So, I tried again. I look into his face once again, to see him speak of what he read on the paper. She wants this thing out of her; he said. I was happy to see that he understood what I had written. I continue writing, trying to persuade the staff to take this thing out, assuring them that I can breath on my own, now. I also needed to know why, I'm tied to this bed? So that you won't harm yourself; the nurse says. Why would I do that? I respond. Please take this out, I ask. Their response was; they had to be sure that I can breath on my own by running some sort of test. I had to calm myself because I had no idea if the police was on the other side of that door.

I turn to my son, I can't help but feel sadness for him as he sits as if waiting for instructions from me. I never wanted my children to see me in this state. I've always been a force to be reckoned with, I am now, reduced to this. I can see that he's worried but trying to keep cool about it. One hour later, they have pulled the tube from my throat, it is suggested that I not speak, to give my throat time to heal and the first thing that I did, was speak. What was the reason that I had to be bound? I ask. The nurse walked to the computer, that was next to my bed and began to type. Basically, you were flailing aggressively, she said. Why would I do that? Apparently, this happened when you were revived, she added. As if, I died? Yes, you were revived in the ambulance outside of your residence and when you were brought back, this is what happened, she said, as she turned to look at me. So, I was fighting for my life? I said in a low tone, basically talking to myself, trying to visualize what I've just been told. Can you take these off please. I'm not a violent person, I said; in a humbling voice. She immediately left the room to return with a male nurse. I watched as the two of them removed the restraints together. I looked around them, to see if the police would rush in but no one did.

I was released on January 2nd of 2024, with a host of instructions and an explanation as to what happened to me. Apparently I had an allergic reaction to a seasoning that I added to the popcorn. It had the ingredient Turbinado sugar in it. I could not believe that there was a seasoning that could kill a person. What was even crazier, I was unaware that I had any allergies at all. Jamie made it to the hospital twenty minutes after I called him. The ride to his home was quiet. I couldn't help but think about everything that happened, it was on repeat in my mind. The things that I don't recall happening, I found myself struggling trying to remember. I ask questions, trying to fill in the gaps but I guess he could only give me what he could remember. As we pulled up into the driveway, he sit for a moment. I'm upset with you ma, he said. Why? Because, this happened here, he said, while bowing his head.

I felt the pain shoot through my eye and travel to my head. It was hard to keep my face together after hearing his words. But, I understood. My God, I understood. His feelings were valid. What happened must have been very traumatic for him, weather he admitted it or not. What he explained was a lot to take in. The fighting and clawing at Elise, whom I don't even remember seeing out there. I tried to keep the bulk of what was going to happen, from the younger ones by sending them upstairs; I thought. Maybe, I should have braced the adults from this as well. But then, I would have surely died, I thought. As he and I walked in the door, the feeling of what I experienced was taking it's tole on me. I hear the grand babies in the other room. As I walk in further, I now see them playing. My ability to acknowledge them was wavering. I wanted to go upstairs to avoid interaction for a while, just until I got my shit together. I smile at them, as I place my foot on the stair and begin the climb. Once in the bedroom, I began gathering my things for the flight home. In the process, the babies came up and began flipping on the bed, I smiled as I watched. Granna, where are you going? Home baby; I answered. Already? He ask. Yes baby, but not until tomorrow, OK. OK, he said, as he jumped on the bed. When finished, I went downstairs to be around the rest of the family. I was overwhelmed with thoughts. I felt out of sorts as I gathered my microphones and boxed them up. When my son walked into the room, I ask if he could please get me a flight out for tomorrow. Why, ma. It's time to go dear, I said calmly. You know that you don't have to go; he added. I need to go, son.

The Uber ride to the airport, was a 45 minute long. I was consumed with thoughts, as to why I was allowed to live. Wondering, what's left in life for me to do? My thoughts were all over the place as I ride the rest of the way, trying to remain calm. Finally arriving in South Bend. If only those that I've smiled at in passing, knew what I had endured only two day ago, I thought. As I turn the key to the house. I stop to look around, thinking that I almost didn't make it back to sit on this porch, or watch people biking, or walking their dogs or even running for that matter. I began to get emotional and then angry about it all. This truly traumatizing episode, has left me, all messed up inside.

When I returned to work that Monday, I felt out of sorts. I walked through the building worrying, if this thing would happen here at my job. I also worried if the Epi Pens that I was given, would work or if I would even be able to stick myself with it. I began to get angry again, I needed a release, someone to talk too, who would have words of encouragement. As the day passed, I pretty much stayed to myself, for fear that I wouldn't or couldn't be my usual self around them. I was still holding on to this anger, as if it were a bad habit. Mad, because I didn't see the bright lights or hear the trumpets or voices from those past on. It was only darkness, and that's it? This made me sad because I expected so much more when I died. I felt betrayed. All of these years of being a christian and listening to my elders preach on this very subject. I felt that if I would live by the code of showing love and doing good by people, that I would have earned this. And then, there was this enormous medical bill that was about to be dropped in my lap from spending two days in the ICU with all of this equipment hooked up to me. Yes, I was angry. I had a conversation with my dear friend Maria, whom I've known and worked with for 19 years. I told her everything, while at work. Her words were kind, loving and gentle, reminding me, that I made it through the storm and now I have to let my light shine as I've always done. I am truly grateful for her words of wisdom.

As days rush by, my anger subsides. My thoughts aren't so much about the past anymore but of issues of the present that hovers over us in the form of a dark cloud. My job is suffering and to our surprise it's not because of our performance. We are part of a large conglomerate and as a whole, we suffer. As, there is nothing that we can do, physically, I fall on bended knee and give it all to God. I literally give everything to god now a days, because there is nothing that I can control in Mi Vida Loca.

The End

End Note

I would love to give you a fairy tale ending. But that doesn't exist in my world, the real world. I am a work in progress. I live each day as if, my last. I have no excuses, or explanations, nor do I feel remorse for the things that have happened in my past. I've prayed about it and let it go. I've learned all that I needed too, to successfully navigate my way through life. I feel as if I'm living on borrowed time so, I am diligent in maintain the connection with those of my children, who wants it. My grandchildren's mothers, are very important to me. They keep me in touch with the babies in their growth and every major milestone in their little lives. I have committed myself to flying to see those who live in Texas. I am also, committed to seeing those children, that are here, near me. While, still traveling, writing and attending functions here in South Bend/ Mishawaka area. I find that supporting different people and their craft or brands, is a way of networking and getting to know some very prominent people in the community. I stray away from negativity and chaos. I value my peace. I'm not quite sure as to why I was brought back to life but I feel as if I am to continue to spread the goodness of God as he has presented himself in my life. I am very aware as to why I am, who I am. However, I am no longer a victim, I stand as a survivor. I am a 59 ½ year old woman that has no desire to step back into a classroom but has learned a many valuable life lessons, along the way. If I had it to do again, would I? HELL NAW! If I had the power to rewrite my story, I would definitely change the narrative, the past is a very tricky place to hang out at. My life is good, now. I could wish for better but I have all that is intended for me to have, at this moment. I've often thought, if I could have just enough money to help everyone that I want to help, and still have enough for myself, life would be great. So, I help who I can now, and still have what's for me. As for my extended family, I keep them in my prayers. WE ALL GOT A STORY TO TELL!

GOD BLESS, ALL WHO READS THESE BOOKS

Made in the USA
Monee, IL
06 November 2024